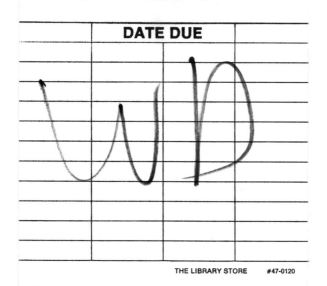

		DATE DUE	

THE LIBRARY STORE   #47-0120

A Teen
Eating Disorder
Prevention
Book

Understanding Weight and Depression

Julie M. Clarke and Ann Kirby-Payne

THE ROSEN PUBLISHING GROUP, INC.
NEW YORK

Published in 2000 by The Rosen Publishing Group, Inc.
29 East 21st Street, New York, NY 10010

First Edition

Library of Congress Cataloging-in-Publication Data

Clarke, Julie M.
    Understanding weight and depression/ Julie M. Clarke and Ann Kirby-Payne.
        p. cm.— (A teen eating disorder prevention book)
    Includes bibliographical references and index.
    Summary: Describes the complexities of eating disorders— anorexia, bulimia, and compulsive eating— as they relate to the psychological illnesses of depression.
    ISBN 0-8239-2992-9
    1. Eating disorders— Juvenile literature. 2. Depression, Mental— Juvenile literature. [1. Eating disorders. 2. Depression, Mental.] I. Kirby-Payne, Ann II. Title. III. Series.
    RC552.E18C52 1999   99-54520

                                                                        CIP
                                                                        AC

Manufactured in the United States of America

ABOUT THE AUTHORS

Julie M. Clarke is a certified social worker at Saint Peter's Medical Center in New Brunswick, New Jersey. She received a Masters of Social Work degree from Rutgers University.

Ann Kirby-Payne is a writer and editor who lives and works in New York City. A graduate of The State University of New York, The College at New Paltz, she is also the author of *Refuse to Use: A Girl's Guide to Drugs and Alcohol.*

ACKNOWLEDGMENTS

Our warmest appreciation to the women and men who have shared their struggles with weight and depression with us over the years. Thanks always to our men and boys: Kevin, Connor, and Kieran Clarke, and Danyal Payne.

Contents

Introduction   **7**

1. Body and Mind   **11**

2. The Body Myth:
   Body Image vs. Body Reality   **24**

3. Danger in the Diet Zone   **46**

4. What Are Eating Disorders?   **72**

5. Depression   **96**

6. Preventing Suicide   **117**

7. Living Healthy, Living Happy   **126**

   Glossary   **134**

   Where to Go for Help   **136**

   For Further Reading   **139**

   Index   **141**

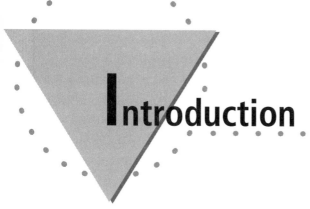

Introduction

*"**L**ook at my gut—I'm huge!"*

"Whenever I'm depressed, I crave chocolate."

"My arms are so scrawny."

"I keep dieting, and I keep failing. I get so disappointed that I just eat, and I wind up gaining weight instead of losing it."

"I know that if I just lost ten pounds, I'd be so much happier."

"There is nothing that scares me as much as getting fat."

The way we see ourselves—and the way we think that we appear to others—can play a big role in the way we act and the way we feel. When we feel good about the way that we look, we feel confident, self-assured, and happy. But when we feel bad about the way we look—which is more often the case—we can feel depressed, alone, unwanted.

TRUTH AND LIES

We all know that beauty is only skin deep, but appearances affect us nonetheless. In our society, messages about appearance, especially about our weight, are constantly forcing us to evaluate our bodies. "Lose weight fast," says one ad; "flat abs in thirty days" says another. The movies we watch feature actors and actresses whose body types are representative of less than 10 percent of the population.

Continuously bombarded with these messages, we begin to believe that being fat is bad; that losing weight is easy; that those of us who are overweight and are unable to lose weight—what with all these fast and easy solutions available—are worthless and lazy. The overarching message is that it is impossible to possess a large body and be happy. And although that message is not true, it has become something of a self-fulfilling prophesy. People who are overweight—even only slightly overweight—often believe that they would be happier if they were thinner.

These are not real beliefs, but they are nonetheless taken to heart by many people. Adolescents are especially susceptible to these lies. During the teen years, our relationships with our changing bodies become strained. Every new development—a pound, an inch—is a potential hazard that must be scrutinized and dealt with. *Am I too short? Too tall? Too thin? Too fat? Do I look like a weakling? Do I look like the Pillsbury Doughboy?* During this time of our lives, when we are trying to figure out who we are and how we fit into the world, we become extremely self-critical, and our bodies are the quickest and easiest targets. If we are not satisfied with the way we look, we may see our disappointment manifested in our feelings about our personalities as well. We may begin to believe the messages we receive every day: *I am fat, I am lazy, I am worthless.*

Our constant and often failed attempts to change the way we look—most often by losing weight, although in some cases by gaining it—can wreak havoc on our psychological well-being. We may find ourselves obsessed with our weight, believing we are fat when we are not. We might develop an eating disorder or an unhealthy obsession with exercise. Or we might find ourselves unable to control ourselves around food, eating compulsively even when we are not hungry. Often poor body image and the lack of self-esteem, which usually comes with it, can lead to depression. Among teens, depression is a particularly frightening and lonely proposition. Serious depression is often ignored by family and friends who attribute it to "growing pains," the normal hardships of the adolescent years. But for many teens, these growing pains become much more than that—they bring on complete despair, perhaps even suicide.

ABOUT THIS BOOK

This book is meant to provide teens with a look at the realities of weight and depression. It provides a guide to the different kinds of disorders that can result from or be influenced by poor or distorted body image. Because you are constantly being faced with unrealistic images of physical beauty, this book also provides facts and theories that you can use to become an educated and critical consumer of information, so that you can be aware of the differences between the "ideal" and the "unreal." Learn to identify signs of depression and eating disorders, and where to turn when you think you or someone close to you needs help. Learn, too, that being healthy and happy does not necessarily mean being thin.

This book also provides guidance for developing a positive body image and setting realistic and healthy goals for your weight and appearance. Accepting and loving your body is just about one of the best things you can do for yourself.

1

Body and Mind

*M*itch is a big guy. He is overweight by any standard; he inherited his father's big frame, and although he eats a healthy diet, he has a tremendous appetite. Yet he has never even tried to take off weight. Since his dad is big, it never occurred to Mitch that there is anything wrong with his size. He is captain of his school's rugby team, very popular with girls, and has lots of friends. He is confident and thinks of himself as handsome and attractive.

Eddie is in Mitch's chemistry class. He is also overweight but lacks the confidence that comes so easily to Mitch. Eddie admires Mitch's attitude and secretly wishes he had the guts to get involved in sports. But the thought of performing any kind of sport with everyone staring at him scares him. How, Eddie wonders, can Mitch manage to forget about the fact that he is fat? How can Mitch talk to girls, play on the field, even sing in the school play, without

11

worrying about what everyone thinks of his body? Such fears of scrutiny have kept Eddie from everything from joining the debate club to attending school dances. Eddie just can't understand how Mitch manages to be happy, even though he's fat.

How closely related are the way we look and the way we feel? Is a lean and healthy athlete more happy than someone who is overweight? Does being thin bring satisfaction? Are all those overweight people miserable, lonely, and depressed, whereas thin people are happy, satisfied, and confident?

HEALTHY APPEARANCES

Happiness should not be connected to our weight, but because of the emphasis our society puts on physical appearance, it often seems as though it is. Advertisements, movies, perhaps even our families and friends are constantly telling us that we cannot be satisfied with our body unless it is as thin as that of a supermodel or athlete. We often mistake thinness for good health and attractiveness for happiness, when in truth they are rarely if ever connected. However, the message that these things are connected is so strong that many people believe it.

The truth is that appearance and health are connected, but not in the ways that we are often led to believe. The thinnest girl at school may be starving herself. Her emaciated figure is a sure sign of some unhealthy psychological problems as well as the fact that her body is suffering from a lack of nutrition. The biggest, strongest boy on the football team may be obsessed with improving his physique to compensate for a horrible sense of inferiority. He fears that is weak, and so becomes obsessed with making himself strong.

THE BEST OF TIMES, THE TOUGHEST OF TIMES

Clarice's family moved the summer before ninth grade, and she headed into high school in fear. For the past eight years, she attended the same small school with the exact same students. She had been confident and self-assured. She had friends whom she knew liked her and students who she didn't like but could at least talk to. The boys in her class she had known since kindergarten. They were almost like brothers. Back home in this comfortable, familiar atmosphere, she had been popular and well liked: a member of the student council, a favorite of teachers and students alike. She played basketball, even though she was not very good, sang in chorus, and acted in plays. She had fun.

But suddenly, here she was, thrown in with a bunch of strangers in a new town. As she walked down the hall, she saw that so many of the girls were so much taller than she, so much thinner, so much more fashionable. They talked to the boys with an easy confidence and casual flirtation. Clarice began to feel tiny, ugly, awkward. When she passed a crowd of busily chatting sophomores, she slouched down, eyes on the floor, and prayed they wouldn't notice her

*shabby shoes, boring haircut, thick glasses, or
the way that her thighs rubbed together when
she walked.*

Your teenage years are a time of excitement,
exploration, and growth. Adolescence is essentially
the time when you come into your own, when you
leave your childhood behind you and step into adulthood. But of course, it's not as simple as stepping
out of one pair of shoes and into another. Becoming
an adult involves not only dealing with growing up
emotionally but also growing up physically. Your
body is changing at the same time your mind is
expanding. Amid these changes, you naturally
become more aware of your body, and your appearance begins to directly affect your feelings and
thoughts. Conversely, your emotions can affect your
appearance and health. The result is an emotional
and physical roller coaster that can be fun but also
terrifying. The twists and turns may give you a thrill,
but they can just as easily make you sick.

For someone like Clarice, who had never felt
awkward or shy before, being the new kid at school
made her terribly self-aware. When faced with students who were already well versed in the ways of
high school and who enjoyed the same kind of secu-
rity she had felt at her own school, Clarice began to
question things she had never felt uncomfortable
with before: her body, her attitude, her clothes.

What Am I turning into?

Have you looked into the mirror lately and wondered,
"What is going on with my body?" Are your arms
suddenly looking a little too long? Are you suddenly

taller than your mom? Are you self-conscious in a tight sweater, feeling too thin and lanky if you are a boy, or if you are a girl, wondering if those new breasts are too big or too small? And hey, wait a minute, is that hair down there?

From the age of about twelve until the age of about seventeen, boys and girls go through a metamorphosis, which could rival a caterpillar's transformation into a butterfly. Your body, which during childhood was pretty much focused on just growing, has added a new trick to its repertoire. Now, it's not only growing, it's changing. Suddenly you're not a kid. But then, you're not quite an adult either. So what are you?

Well, you're an adolescent. What does that mean? Technically, it means you are in the period of your life that lasts from puberty until maturity, which is the point at which your culture deems you an adult. At one point in this country, you were considered an adult at eighteen. Nowadays, you are still considered a kid until you are twenty-one. But the point is, you're in the process of growing up. And although your society and culture may determine when the process ends, there's no question that your body decides when it starts.

The physical changes of adolescence are different from the growth we experience as children in a few very important ways. Whereas before you were getting merely taller or stronger, now your body is becoming more manly or womanly. Suddenly, the girls and boys in your class aren't built the same way. This is no coincidence of nature. These changes are brought on by a raging sea of new hormones that have been released into your body.

They make you not only look more manly or womanly, they make you feel that way too.

Things are changing inside your body and outside of it. At times, you might feel a little awkward in your body, as though you're wearing someone else's clothes and they don't quite fit. Similarly, those hormones are sending some new emotions through your body. Girls start finding themselves coping with the monthly surge of hormones that can wreak havoc on their moods, along with the physical cramps that often accompany menstruation. And the boys don't have it any easier, faced with new and unusual sexual urges, living in fear of being caught with an inappropriate bulge at the front of their jeans.

These physical changes are natural and normal. They can be embarrassing, even humiliating, but they are part of the bittersweet story of adolescence, and you should take comfort in the fact that every adult has already gone through it, and every little kid will have to deal with it someday. But the changes don't end with your body. Something, it seems, is also changing the way that you think and feel.

Who Am I Turning Into?

In much the same way that your body is changing, your thoughts, opinions, feelings, and attitudes are changing as well. Part of becoming an adult involves breaking free from your dependence on your parents and family and learning to depend instead on yourself. You need to determine what kind of adult you want to be. This is also a time when you begin to set your own rules. As children, we pretty much adhere to the rules our parents set out for us, but as we come into adolescence, we begin to decide for ourselves what we like, what we dislike; how we will behave; what we will and will not do. It is also during this time that we begin to set our own priorities about what is important in our lives and set our own standards of what is good, bad, ugly, and beautiful.

At the heart of adolescence is a process known as self-definition. Self-definition refers to our attempts to determine who we are on our own terms. As children, we were defined by our parents, siblings, and teachers. During our adolescent years, we want to determine who we are—as well as what we hope to be and how we will get there—for ourselves.

Peer Influence

One of the dramatic realities of adolescence is peer pressure, or to use a more accurate phrase, peer influence. Our need to be accepted, respected, or at least acknowledged by our fellow teens can some-times play a role in determining our behavior.

When we hear about peer pressure, most often its in relation to drugs, alcohol, and other obviously bad behavior. But the opinions, actions, and exam-ples of our friends and fellow teens affect our lives in many ways that go far beyond the easily under-stood threats of drugs and drinking. From the clothes we wear to the subjects we study, our actions and thoughts are almost always influenced by those around us in some way. Sometimes the role of peer influence is obvious, as when we take slack for turning down a drink or a smoke at a weekend party or we join in dangerous behavior because we fear the disapproval of our friends. On the positive side, gaining the respect or encouragement of our peers often inspires us to great things, from striving for higher grades to finishing a tough obstacle course during Phys Ed class.

An important part of the process of self-definition involves turning away from the choices, goals, and expectations that our parents and others have set for us. But we are new at making these decisions for ourselves. We are used to having someone else to use as a guide. So we invariably turn to our peers for guidance. We begin to set our own style, our own standards for beauty, brains, everything, with a little help from our friends.

DISEASES OF THE MIND—AND BODY

There are many psychological disorders that are rooted in or connected to our weight or our own conception of our physical appearance. Depression and eating disorders are serious psychological conditions that can be connected to our feelings about how we look. In a society that values thinness, overweight people are made to feel worthless, which can cause feelings of depression.

Such feelings are especially prevalent in teens who are just beginning to come to terms with their bodies. At a time when looks are very important, teens dissatisfied with their appearance can be overly critical of themselves. Self-conscious and depressed, many teens, especially girls, become obsessed with their weight. They turn to dieting, exercise, even abusing laxatives and diet drugs in an endless search for a thinner body. Their own view of their body can become distorted, leading them to believe that they are overweight, fat, even obese, when in fact they are dangerously thin. They may begin an impossible battle with food and develop eating disorders that often prove deadly.

These disorders go far beyond body image and an obsessive desire to be thin. Another type of eating disorder is compulsive eating. Rather than being enemies of food, victims of compulsive eating disorders become slaves to it. They eat more than they need to, hoping that the food will satisfy their emotions the way that it satisfies their stomachs. They find themselves eating even when they are not hungry at all—eating out of boredom, habit, or because of a deep, insatiable desire to keep eating that is as unhealthy and yet as real as the anorexic's need to lose weight. They face the horrible health risks that invariably accompany obesity. They also face the scorn of a society that frowns upon fat, that shuns those who are unable to control their appetites and their weight.

Depression seems to be a common thread that eating disorder sufferers share. Sometimes depression accompanies an eating disorder. Other times, it rears its ugly head all alone. Victims find themselves unable to feel happy about anything, and their despair can lead to desperation. They may wind up abusing drugs, engaging in dangerous sexual or physical behaviors, even intentionally hurting themselves. In extreme cases, victims of depression may consider—even attempt—to end their own lives. They often succeed.

SCARS THAT DON'T HEAL

Monique has a secret.

When she was ten years old, a strange man grabbed her on her way home from school. He pulled her into a dark alley and held a knife to her throat. As he pulled up the skirt of her school uniform, he told her that if she screamed, he would slit her throat. Then he raped her. "Don't cry," he told her in an angry, hateful voice. "Someday you'll be all grown up, and you'll think this is fun."

She never told a soul. But she never, ever forgot. As she headed into adolescence, she found herself very afraid. She feared losing her childlike figure, terrified of becoming the "woman" her attacker spoke of. When breasts started to sprout on her chest, she started wearing large sweatshirts. She found herself obsessed with her appearance, checking the mirror and the scale every day. "Am I taller? Am I bigger? Are my hips getting wide?"

Take a look at all the girls and guys in your class. Chances are, most of them have a secret or two. Some, like Monique's, may be so devastating that they cannot ever tell a soul. They bury them just under the surface and battle against them every day. Others may have experienced untold traumas that range from being beaten up by the school bully to being abandoned by a parent. These painful events, be they serious or merely embarrassing, take an undeniable toll on our lives. We grow, we learn, we adapt, but we never forget. From the biggest traumas to the smallest, you will undoubtedly find that your childhood is not that easy to leave behind, and the scars of painful memories will remain with you and affect the choices you make as you develop into an adult.

Monique's horrible secret may affect her life in any number of ways. As her appearance becomes more womanly, she may direct the anger she feels over her experience toward her body. She may starve it in an attempt to remain more childlike in appearance. She may overfeed it in an attempt to disguise it. She may not be able to see past her own sadness and may begin to hate herself, to abuse herself, to toy with the idea of ending her own life. Or she may learn to talk about her problem, to seek help, to find closure to the horrible episode that has haunted her since she was ten years old.

If you have suffered a major trauma in your life, it is important not to keep it a secret. Talk to an adult you trust or contact one of the organizations listed at the end of this book. If you take action now, you will be taking the first step toward preventing dangerous or self-destructive behaviors.

Understanding Eating Disorders and Depression

Psychological problems like depression and eating disorders are very complicated. Entire libraries could be and have been written about each of them. Unlike most physical disorders, they cannot be blamed on one simple culprit: a germ, an accident, or a bad reaction to a chemical or drug. Psychological disorders are more often a complex reaction to many causes, ranging from the genetic material we inherit from our parents, grandparents, and other ancestors to the physical environment that surrounds us, and to the unique experiences that we go through during our lives.

There is no one cause for any psychological disorder, and even the most prominent researchers are only beginning to understand the many ways in which eating disorders and depression can develop. There are countless theories on the root causes of these problems and also many theories on how they develop and how they can be treated.

But there is one thing that is certain: These disorders are real. They begin in the mind, but they manifest themselves in the body. They are diseases of the psyche that often prove harmful—even fatal—to life itself. But they don't have to get that far. By reading this book and educating yourself about weight and depression, you may be able to prevent an eating disorder from setting in or help yourself recover from an eating disorder.

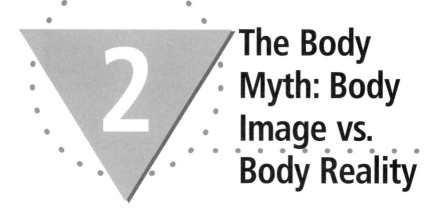

The Body Myth: Body Image vs. Body Reality

E velyn didn't want to go to school. Today her Phys Ed class was going to start swimming, and the thought of having everyone in her class see her in her bathing suit was making her panic. She had been teased about her chubbiness all her life. By the time she was in fifth grade, she had been called enough names to fill a book of insults. When she was younger, she was able to shrug it off, but suddenly it seemed impossible to ignore. There were girls in her gym class who were especially cruel, and she so feared their scrutiny that she was afraid to even attempt to exercise in front of them. In fact, she'd even tried going to the gym after school, but there she had been surrounded by fit, trim girls who made her feel so self-conscious that she left after only a few minutes. She tried dieting as well but always wound up tired and depressed after about a week. What she would have done to have the thin body of her best friend, Vanessa.

Meanwhile, Vanessa was at home, dreading the very same class. Her breasts were too small, her hips were too wide. No matter what she did, she still had a little belly that just wouldn't get flat. She was thin, she knew, but still, her waist was not as small as she wanted it, and her legs were so long and wiry that the boys called her "stilt walker." She biked, worked out with weights, even tried some muscle-building drinks, but no matter what she did, she could not get her body as toned as she felt it should be.

We are a society obsessed with our weight and our bodies. How can we avoid it? Every day, we are bombarded with messages telling us that we are not thin enough, not strong enough, not healthy enough. Sit down for an hour of television, perhaps to watch *Beverly Hills, 90210,* or *Dawson's Creek.* Take a look at the cast. Each woman has a flat, washboard stomach and long, lean legs. Every man has a muscular upper body, arms like an athlete, and no belly to speak of. They wear clothing that emphasizes these traits. The women's skirts are cut unrealistically high, their shirts cropped short to expose their midriffs, and the men seem to go shirtless whenever the mood strikes them. Watching these shows, one might think that anyone with a bit of meat on their bones is a freak.

But it doesn't end there. Between scenes of the shows, you'll be hit with advertisements for everything from fast food to gym equipment. A big, fatty burger will tempt you one moment, and a few minutes later, you'll be told that you've only got eight weeks to get in shape before bathing suit season hits. Diet shakes promise "give us a week, we'll take off the weight," while sneaker advertisements tell you to get out and start running. Meanwhile, it is late on a weeknight—the middle of winter. You look at yourself in the mirror and hate what you see, and you feel depressed. There is no way you're ever going to look like those people on television. You reach for a piece of chocolate cake to make yourself feel a little bit better.

For many men and women, dealing with their own body image can be a daily trial. When they look in the mirror, they are not happy with what they see. In 1997 *Psychology Today* magazine polled 4,000 readers and found that 56 percent of women and 43 percent of men were unhappy with their overall appearance, and over 60 percent of the women and 50 percent of the men were troubled specifically with their weight. We are a nation of dieters, of people completely dissatisfied with our appearance. Young people today are being groomed to fit into a society that places a very high value on physical appearance. Television, movies, fashion magazines, even music present physical ideals that are impossible for most people to attain. It is depressing enough to feel ugly or unattractive as an adult. As an adolescent, it can be devastating.

AN UNREALISTIC IDEAL

Megan, fifteen, is out shopping with her mother and her aunt. She is, according to standards set by doctors, slim and healthy, tipping the scales at just over 105 pounds at five feet, three inches in height. Yet today she stands in the department store, looking in the mirror in disgust. She is trying on a tight-fitting, cropped T-shirt and a long, slim-cut skirt. The same outfit looked awesome on the models in the magazine and on the store mannequin. Yet Megan feels chubby, like a little stuffed sausage. She takes it off and heads off to find something else.

Meanwhile, Megan's mother is in the ladies department, trying on a dress. Turning in front of the mirror, she can't hide her frown. "You know," she tells her sister, "twenty years ago, I could wear anything. I would try on a dress and look as good as any fashion model. It's weird . . . I haven't really gotten any bigger since I was twenty-five, even after having a child—my weight and measurements are exactly the same as they were when I was in college. But somehow, my body just isn't the same."

What's So Super About Models?

Why is it that clothing rarely looks as good on you as it does on a model? How do those models keep their bellies so flat? And how come clothing that looks so cool on them often looks disproportioned, dumpy, or just plain bad when we try it on?

The simple fact is that models' bodies are different than most people's. They are almost always taller than average, and much thinner than average. They are usually slim because of dieting and exercise, but sometimes they are thinner because that is the way their genetic code is programmed. Being thin is as normal and natural for them as being tall.

But most people are not so thin naturally. Only 5 percent of females in the United States naturally possess the model's type of body. And although fashion models have been slimmer than average for many years, in the past twenty years, the weight gap between the average woman and the average model has widened substantially. Today's models are 23 percent thinner than the average American woman. Twenty years ago models were only 8 percent thinner than average.

Yet clothing and advertising are almost always geared toward making women think that they should look like models. This is why slim Megan feels stout when she tries on the outfit she admired in the fashion magazine. She is shorter than a model so the skirt and top designed for a model's long form makes her look stubby. It is also why Megan's mom isn't happy with her choice. Her body, which had been the ideal twenty years before, is no longer the model type. She has stayed the same, but the models have gotten thinner.

Changing Standards of Beauty and Attractiveness

There is a saying that one can never be too rich or too thin. Today the idealized image of success is usually accompanied by a slender, rail-thin figure for women, a muscular, toned body for men. Fat is seen as a sign of sloppiness, or lack of work and motivation, even of poverty. But rewind fifty, one hundred, two hundred years and take a look at the women and men who were considered ideal body types in those times. You might be quite surprised.

Once upon a time, thin bodies, muscular torsos, and tanned skin were all features of the lower working classes. Wealthy aristocrats, kings and queens, and noblepeople took pride in their wide bellies, their double chins, and their pale, nearly translucent flesh. These were signs of success and wealth, signs that these people did not need to engage in physical labor the way poorer people did. Like today's models and movie stars, the upper classes of yesterday set the standard for beauty and attractiveness. For most of modern history, a plump body—unhealthy and unattractive by today's standards—was considered ideal.

Why is it that today, things seem to be just the reverse? Most Americans today are somewhat to very overweight, and the movie stars, models, and athletes who set our standards for beauty and attractiveness are thin, muscular, often even underweight. We have become a nation of dieters, often moving from one unhealthy fad diet to another, spending millions on exercise equipment, and most of us never really attain or maintain a healthy weight.

Let's Go to the Movies:
A Lesson in Comparative History

Marilyn Monroe was the sex symbol of the 1950s and is still considered one of the sexiest, most attractive women who ever lived. She was the woman men most desired and other women wanted to look like. Monroe, along with other femme fatales like Jane Russell, Betty Grable, and Jayne Mansfield, set the standards for womanliness and beauty, much like Naomi Campbell and Christy

Turlington do today. So let's try an experiment. Let's compare Marilyn Monroe with the celebrity most often compared to her today, Madonna. Go to your local video store and rent a classic Monroe flick like *The Seven Year Itch* or *Bus Stop*. Watch it and then think about Marilyn's body in comparison to Madonna's.

Marilyn, you'll see, was curvaceous and even plump. She had wide hips and round, full breasts, and her arms, belly, and legs were, by today's standards, soft and fat. Madonna has, throughout her career, showed off a slim, muscular figure. She sports the kind of flat stomach that few women can hope for. Her arms are strong and show the results of a great deal of time spent working out. Next to Marilyn, she might look a bit scrawny. And healthy, athletic Madonna is not an underweight, malnourished-looking supermodel. Next to Kate Moss or Naomi Campbell, Marilyn Monroe—one of the most idolized women in history—might look positively obese.

If you think this kind of change in ideal is only something women have to deal with, think again. Males, too, have to deal with changing standards of attractiveness. Although traditionally they have been less prone to poor self-esteem in regards to their bodies, recent studies show that the pressure on men to be thin, muscular, and strong is growing. Once again, let's take a trip to the video store for a quick lesson in changing standards. Rent one of the classic Tarzan films, starring Johnny Weismuller, and a comparable film from recent years, perhaps *George of the Jungle* with Brendan Frazer. Both films depict men raised in the jungle, and both stars present the standard for male physiques for their times. But next to Brendan's lean and muscular chest and washboard abs, poor Johnny Weismuller—the buffest guy in 1930s Hollywood—looks like the Pillsbury Doughboy.

BODY IMAGE DURING ADOLESCENCE

Our nation's obsession with weight can have devastating consequences for young people. We live in an age when appearance is everything and billion-dollar industries have been built around making people chase after a nearly impossible goal: thinness.

During adolescence, our bodies are changing, and we are in the process of learning to behave, act, and think like adults. It is also the time of our lives when we are the most self-conscious as our changing bodies present us with a daily challenge. As we change into men and women, we are painfully aware of our expanding hips and broadening chests. Our appearance becomes a huge indicator of who we are. Nobody wants to be the shortest or the tallest. Nobody wants to be the fattest or the thinnest. As we become interested in dating, we become more intrigued by our own attractiveness. Often we become very critical of ourselves and of others. These natural changes, combined with the messages we receive constantly from the media, our parents, teachers, and from just about everywhere, can often result in a poor body image.

Poor body image can start in early childhood and often gets worse during adolescence when young people are most concerned with their changing and developing bodies. During the crucial years from the ages of about eleven to seventeen or a bit later, we watch our bodies grow and change and adjust our attitudes and behaviors as we grow. Poor attitudes toward our bodies during adolescence can have serious consequences later on.

In a society that places such high value on appearance, and especially on thinness, prejudices have invariably arisen toward people who are overweight. People who are overweight are often perceived as being lazy, self-indulgent, or as having no self-control. People who suffer from being overweight often come to believe these myths. They begin to see themselves as lazy slobs, and they begin to hate themselves. This kind of self-hatred is often unfounded. Many people are overweight despite healthy diet and exercise habits, and many people suffer from obesity because of real glandular disorders or heredity. Even worse, many people who consider themselves overweight are not, but they suffer the same kind of self-hate because they do not measure up to the unrealistic ideals set forth by the media.

WHAT'S WEIGHING YOU DOWN?

Many adolescents suffer from a poor body image. They look in the mirror, and rather than taking a fair assessment of their bodies, they see only negative features. A girl with long, attractive legs will see only her protruding tummy. A boy with a lean athletic frame will wish his shoulders were broader. Although it is normal to see areas that need improvement, those suffering from poor body image will never see anything positive. Their skewed attitudes can be partially blamed on the modern ideal of unrealistically thin or muscular frames, but there are many other factors that can contribute to poor body image.

Those who gain weight suddenly, who are teased about their weight, or who have been raised to be extremely conscious of their weight often develop an unrealistically negative attitude toward their bodies.

Names Can Harm You

"Hey, Fatsy!" the boys would call out when Patsy got on the school bus. Patsy would just look at the floor and try to find a seat without making eye contact with anyone. "Aim for Fatsy!" the girls would shout during dodgeball games. "She's a big easy target." Patsy would try to fake being sick every day for gym, but she rarely got away with it. She dreaded going to school each day, dreaded even walking out of the door of her house. "You're not fat," her mother would tell her. "You're just a bit bigger than the other girls . . . don't worry, you'll outgrow it."

Remember teasing other kids when you were little? Remember getting teased by other kids? Children can be cruel, no doubt, and teenagers can be even more cruel. We have all suffered some sharp, mean words at some time or another. Kids with glasses, speech impediments, disabilities, even kids with unusual coloring—freckles, for example—are almost always called names and teased. It always hurts, but we get over it in time.

Or do we? In many ways, we carry the scars of teasing our whole lives. Look at Patsy. Do you think you could take that kind of torture? Do you think you would get over it easily? People who are overweight suffer from all kinds of cruelties. Sometimes they do indeed outgrow their weight problems as Patsy's mother suggested. But they carry the stigma of being fat for the rest of their lives.

Patsy, in fact, did outgrow her pudginess. By the time she was thirteen, she had gotten quite tall and slim. But the sting of the taunts she received in elementary school continue to haunt her. Now a thin fifteen-year-old, she still sees herself as being fat. When she walks past a crowd of girls, she always thinks that they are whispering about her. She weighs herself weekly to make sure that she is not gaining weight. She watches her diet like a hawk.

Similarly, eighteen-year-old Carlos was the victim of taunts and as a result is terribly afraid of gaining weight. What's strange is that Carlos himself has never been overweight. His mother, however, is very large, and has struggled with obesity for many years. As a child and as a teen, Carlos has endured the snickering of children and many adults who would comment on his mother's weight, making nasty jokes and whispering cruelly when she walked him to school. As a result, Carlos became obsessed with staying thin at an exceptionally young age and carried his fear of fat with him for his whole life.

Poor body image can also be expressed aggressively. Consider Kirsten, a sixteen-year-old who, though overweight as a child, has grown into an active and fit teenager. She does not find it difficult to stay slim, but she knows that she must keep exercising regularly and always watches what she eats. Like Patsy, she was teased and taunted as a child. But unlike Patsy, who is now overly critical of herself, Kirsten is overly critical of others. In fact, she is the harshest girl in school, always scrutinizing the other girls in her class and passing cruel remarks to those she deems "fat." One would think that someone who has endured such remarks would be sensitive to others' feelings. But the reality is that Kirsten knows she could be fat, and she sees herself in those overweight girls. She fears becoming fat so much that she tries to distance herself from it. She tortures the girls who are not able to win the fight against fat in order to show that she is not like them, that she is a winner.

We have all seen people teased about their weight. Many of us have been victims of that kind of teasing. Still others may have even participated in the teasing. Most of us outgrow it, but for people with weight problems, this kind of teasing never ends. Although the rules of political correctness have at long last put an end to making fun of people with disabilities or who belong to ethnic or racial minorities, it is still considered permissible to make fun of people who are fat. Consider the depictions of plump little Bobby Hill on the popular animated sitcom *King of the Hill* or the constant string of fat jokes aimed at Drew and Mimi on *The Drew Carey Show.* Stereotypes of overweight people as being obsessed with food are common. Large people are also often presented as being lazy, sloppy, and as having absolutely no self-control. These images might provide a laugh or two at the movie theater, but they are not founded in reality, and they cause a great deal of pain for many people who struggle with their weight.

A Family Affair

"Don't you worry about what those kids say," Michael's mother said as she handed him another piece of cake, "you are not overweight!" Michael sighed again. Every time he tried to turn down a second serving of potatoes or said he didn't want dessert, his mother went ballistic. At sixteen, he was severely overweight and had been listening to taunts of "fatso" and "wide load" ever since he'd started school. He desperately wanted to lose a little weight—just enough so that he could feel confident enough to talk to girls—but his mother simply would not hear it. "Eat your dinner," she always said sweetly, "and leave a little room for dessert . . . I made your favorite chocolate cake!"'

Problems with weight and food often run in families. Many people are genetically programmed to be larger or to have a tendency toward being overweight. These genetic predispositions are often supported by the lifestyles we inherit from our parents and other family members. Meals are a social event, and we learn our attitudes about food from our families just as surely as we learn to speak.

Michael's mother uses food to express her love for her son. She is in denial of the fact that Michael is overweight. He has a real problem with his weight, but she has concocted her own body image for him. She simply refuses to accept that her son is overweight. Part of this is because she can only see her son as perfect, the way that many parents see their children. But another part of her problem is that his obesity has been caused—at least in part—by her own choice of expressing her love through food. Michael cannot deny the food because that would be denying his mother's love.

Parents can also pass down their own insecurities to their children. A parent with a poor body image will often pass that trait down to his or her child. Michelle's mother, for example, struggled with her weight as a young girl. She has raised Michelle to be extremely self-conscious about her own weight even though Michelle has never been overweight at all. Michelle, at seventeen, is twenty pounds underweight and is still convinced that she is fat.

Meanwhile, Back at the Playground . . .

Melody and Angela stood in the schoolyard, discussing their diets. "I'm eating nothing but fruit today," Melody stated proudly. "I did that three days last week, and I lost five pounds." Angela agreed. "That's right," she said. "I did the same thing for four days in a row this week, and I'm already four pounds thinner."

Wendy looked at them, astonished. Melody and Angela were the coolest girls in the seventh grade, and more than anything, Wendy wanted to be accepted into their clique. But Wendy didn't understand why all they talked about was dieting. They were already perfectly thin. They were way skinnier than her. Come to think of it, they looked a little too skinny like maybe a strong breeze could knock them both over. But maybe it is better to be thinner, Wendy thought. She considered her own weight and the large bowl of cereal she had for breakfast. She imagined admitting this to Angela and Melody. She could almost see Angela's expression of disapproval and hear Melody's disgust. "With milk?" they would ask. And then the shame, the horrible shame Wendy would feel as she nodded her head and waited for their unavoidable follow-up question: "Whole milk?"

It is not surprising that problems with our body image usually first pop up during adolescence. We begin to look at ourselves with new standards, standards that are very different from the ones we lived by as children. When we look at ourselves, we see bodies that are rapidly changing and growing in new and perhaps alarming ways. We need to know how to evaluate these strange new bodies, and we do not want to turn to our parents for guidance. So we turn to our friends, even though we may know that our friends are no more prepared or aware than we are. Perhaps they or we ourselves look to magazines, television, and other media outlets to provide the kind guidance that our parents once gave us to help us to evaluate ourselves. The images presented there are, as we have already discussed, not the most realistic place to start.

That's why, at this time when we are making up our minds about our bodies, our images of ourselves often become distorted. Consider the story above about Wendy, who found herself suddenly feeling out of the clique when she imagined that her diet would not meet with the approval of Angela and Melody. The two dieting teens have decided that losing weight is their top priority, that they must obsess over their diet and that essentially they would rather be malnourished than gain weight. Their attitude is completely unhealthy. Growing girls cannot live on nothing but fruit, and at this time in their lives they should be gaining, not losing weight. And Wendy, who respects the other two girls' opinions, has become terribly self-critical, imagining that her healthy breakfast is a poor diet choice. If Wendy gives into the influence of Angela and Melody, she may find herself with an eating disorder and health problems down the line. Angela and Melody, of course, are already there. Hoping to lose weight and essentially starving themselves in order to do so, they have terribly skewed visions of their bodies and, if they do not give up dieting very, very soon, are on the road to anorexia.

BAD ATTITUDES, BAD CONSEQUENCES

Just how common is negative body image? Just how happy are young people today with the way that they look? Consider these startling statistics. Sixty-two percent of teenage girls report being unhappy with their weight, and over 80 percent of fourth-grade girls today are dieting. Surveys show that young girls are more worried about getting fat than they are about nuclear war, cancer, or losing their parents. Although this problem has always been more associated with females than with males, recent studies show that poor body image among boys and men is a problem on the rise.

The desire to be thin is not a desire to be healthy. In fact, when researchers at *Psychology Today* magazine asked men and women if they would trade years for pounds—that is, if they would give up a few years of their life for thinness—24 percent of women and 17 percent of men said that yes, they would trade more than three years of their life in exchange for a thinner body.

Sadly, in many cases, people do just that. Dieting is so common in this country that at any given time, 15 to 35 percent of the population is actively trying to lose weight. Many of them engage in dangerous behavior that has been proven detrimental to health. Some binge and purge, abuse laxatives, or even starve themselves. These eating disorders, anorexia and bulimia, have mortality rates as high as 20 percent. Some people resort to painful and dangerous plastic surgeries to remove fat from their bodies, and more abuse potentially fatal diet drugs in order to lose weight.

But even less drastic methods for losing weight can be dangerous. Dieting itself can be dangerous; many people desperate for a way to lose weight subscribe to dangerous "fad" diets, which do not provide the nutrients they need to stay healthy. These diets often do not work, and when they do, the weight rarely stays off for long. As a result, many people watch their weight "yo-yo." They lose weight quickly and then gain it back again in an unhealthy cycle that can be more detrimental to one's health than obesity ever was. In fact, *The New England Journal of Medicine* recently pointed out that, despite the many health risks of obesity, for many people it is better to remain at their "natural" weight than it is for them to constantly battle to lose weight.

When We Hate What We See

A negative body image may not seem like cause for concern. After all, we all have parts of our bodies that we hate or go through phases where we don't like the way that we look. But having negative attitudes toward our bodies can have very serious and even dangerous consequences.

People who are troubled by their weight often find themselves on an endless cycle of dieting. They try dangerous fad and crash diets that wreak havoc on their systems and watch their weight yo-yo up and down as time goes by. Recent studies show that many women and girls refuse to quit smoking because they are terrified of gaining weight. Some even take up the dangerous habit in hope of losing weight.

Even those with only a moderately bad body image—focusing on just a few "trouble spots"—face serious problems. They may be hesitant to engage in certain activities, and they may find it hard to assert themselves in relationships, at school, and at work. This is because their poor body image makes them terribly self-conscious. They may be afraid to wear a swimsuit or be intimidated by other, more slender people. They can become afraid of doing anything that might draw attention to them, from dancing to raising their hands in class.

Often during adolescence, negative body images take over. Poor attitudes toward physical appearance can eclipse all other attitudes and beliefs and lead to very serious conditions. Poor body image often leads to feelings of worthlessness, the feeling that because you are overweight you will never gain acceptance or happiness. Such feelings of self-consciousness can make teens especially vulnerable to peer pressure. They lack the confidence to make their own decisions and will often follow the crowd blindly in hopes that they will gain acceptance by emulating others' behavior. Teens who hate their bodies will often engage in high-risk behavior, such as experimenting with drugs or alcohol. They are also more likely to engage in unwanted sex or other behaviors that will only damage their self-esteem further.

As negative body image becomes more serious so do its consequences. Serious psychological disorders can develop when body image becomes grossly distorted. As victims of poor body image become more self-conscious, their bodies become the center of their world. Conditions like anorexia nervosa and bulimia nervosa lead victims to develop completely distorted views of their body. They may be just skin and bones, but when they look in the mirror, they see themselves as fat. (Eating disorders will be discussed in depth in chapter four.)

Depression is also common among those with poor body image. As they become more self-conscious, they also become more withdrawn. Those who suffer from being overweight often have to deal with constant teasing and mocking from others. They often make the trauma even worse by being cruel to themselves. They despise their bodies and think of themselves as fat, lazy people, subscribing to the many prejudices that others have applied to them over the years. Their bodies become the single most important thing in their world—the very definition of who they are. When people feel so negatively toward it, the consequences can be harsh. Dieting can make it worse because failed diets will make victims only more depressed. (Depression will be discussed at length in chapter three.)

HOW'S YOUR BODY IMAGE?

During adolescence, it is natural to feel critical of your appearance. One of the most important processes that adolescents go through is defining themselves: that is, determining who you are and what kind of person you want to be. It is natural that during this time you might be critical of yourself. However, if you are dissatisfied with your body to the point that you cannot see any positive aspects of it, you could be in serious trouble.

The exercises that follow are designed to help you assess your own personal body image. Answer them honestly.

- ⊙ How do you define yourself?

- ⊙ When you look in the mirror, what do you see?

- ⊙ Describe your favorite part of your body.

- ⊙ Describe your least favorite part.

- ⊙ Describe how you think other people see you.

Now take a look at your answers.

⊙ Does your definition include aspects of your appearance, and if so, do you use negative terms to describe them (for example, "I am a fat girl," as opposed to "I am a girl")?

⊙ Do you focus only on negative aspects?

⊙ How do you describe the parts of your body that you are unhappy with? Do you use more descriptive words than you used for parts you were satisfied with? For example, did you say, "my arms are ok" for favorite body part, but "my stomach is huge, gross, disgusting" for least favorite?

⊙ Do you go to great pains to try to change the parts of your body that you are unhappy with or to cover them up with baggy clothes?

⊙ Do you think other people notice your bad parts first or notice only bad parts?

If you found yourself being more critical than complimentary, you may have a body image problem. If you are unable to find a single positive thing to say or are unable to muster enough confidence to compliment yourself, you might have serious self-image issues that can affect your confidence, your ability to make good decisions, and your mental and physical health as you grow older.

However, if you were able to make a well-balanced assessment of your body, focusing on the positive and acknowledging but accepting the negative, you have a better and more healthy sense of your body.

3

Danger
in the
Diet Zone

*I*t was two weeks before the junior prom. Candide tried on her dress to see how well it matched the shoes and purse she'd just bought and almost screamed. Why did it look so tight around the waist? Hadn't it fit just fine three weeks ago when she picked it out? She thought back angrily to the trips to the mall she'd taken with her friends, always ending with a trip to the ice cream parlor. And her mother's huge Sunday dinners, with mounds of potatoes and butter. And the hours she'd spent in front of the television, when she could have been out walking, biking, doing something—anything—to keep at least a little bit in shape.

What was she going to do? There was only two weeks, and no amount of running, jogging, or biking was going to make that dress fit right by then. Desperate, she got dressed and headed to the drug store, remembering an advertisement for a product that promised to take off

46

extra pounds in just a week. How hard could it be, she wondered. Have a diet shake for break-fast, another for lunch, and then have a regular dinner with her family. She bought a six-pack of chocolate shakes and a six-pack of vanilla and hoped that would do the trick.

You cannot watch television, read a magazine, even go to the drug store or the supermarket without being bombarded with advertisements and products that promise to give you the body you want with little effort on your part. All you need to do, it seems, is spend some money and follow directions.

BAD BODY IMAGE IS GOOD FOR BUSINESS

Anthony was really looking forward to starting college. He would be in an entirely new city where nobody would know him. For years he had struggled with his weight. He had no confidence with girls and had endured teasing since he was a child. He planned to take the summer to get in shape so that he could start all over in the fall with a new, slim body.

In June, he joined a local weight-loss group. Each week he would meet with a group of other people, all of whom were trying to lose weight. He had a counselor who helped him set a goal weight and develop a meal plan. The food requirements intimidated him. He would have to meticulously control his portions, weighing everything to ensure that he ate only the amount allotted by the plan. What was worse, he could not cook, and he did not want to ask his already-overworked mother to prepare special meals just for him. "It will be easier to control your portion and lose weight if you buy our prepackaged foods," the counselor told him. "They are all ready to eat—just pop them in the microwave—and they are designed to fit the program exactly." Relieved, Anthony purchased a week's worth of meals at the cost of half a week's salary from his summer job— money he was going to need for school.

Excited, Anthony announced that he would not be sharing in the family meal that night. As his parents and brother sat down to a dinner of steak and potatoes, Anthony heated up his frozen entree of low-fat lasagna. The meal was salty yet somewhat flavorless, and there wasn't much of it. He had finished it before his brother even got around to his baked potato. Starving, Anthony reached for the prepared dessert that was part of his plan, despite the fact that his family did not routinely have desserts and wouldn't be eating one that evening. He tried to enjoy the crumbly low-fat brownie, but he was dying to reach out and grab the baked potato off of his brother's plate.

The diet industry is a booming, money-making enterprise. It is estimated that Americans spend $30 to $50 billion each year on weight-loss programs, diet drugs, special foods, gym memberships, and other products and services that supposedly will help them to lose weight. A huge industry has developed that profits from people's insecurities about their weight. Everything from low-fat cookies to huge, expensive pieces of home-exercise equipment is designed to turn a profit. These companies support an unrealistic body image by using ultra-slim models to pitch their products. After all, if the models were shaped like regular people, then regular people would not feel the need to go out and buy their products. So next time you look at a model and feel fat by comparison, remember that this is their job. By making you feel bad about yourself, they inspire you to spend your money on diet products.

Each year, we spend millions of dollars on weight-loss programs, many of which have not been proven to work. Programs like Anthony's require weekly membership fees, along with the cost of their food if you chose to use that instead of preparing your own meals. Other programs are even more costly, requiring you to eat only their expensive prepackaged meals or requiring expensive diet supplements or both. Add to this the costs of gym memberships, home gym equipment, dietary supplements, prescription and over-the-counter diet drugs, and the countless other "cures" for weight problems, and you've got a multimillion dollar industry. Consider Anthony who was spending all his money on a diet that has little chance of success. After his first meal, he's still starving, and chances are, he won't be able to go on like that for long.

Weighing the Costs

The sad truth is that for all the time and money Americans spend in search of a perfect body, the majority of us are still overweight. Although the statistics show that many of us are dieting or have dieted, the truth is that most of us never do manage to take off the extra weight. Why is it that a society of people who are so aware of their bodies are still struggling with their weight?

Much of the problem lies in our inability to recognize how we can be healthy. We are a nation of consumers, and we have been trained from a very young age to believe that if there is something we want, we can buy it. If we want a car, we go to a dealer; if we want longer hair, we can get a weave. So when we want to change our bodies, we look for ways to purchase it: We might purchase a membership at a gym or in a diet program, or perhaps we'll just go down to the bookstore and buy the latest diet book, or to the drugstore to buy a package of diet pills.

There are countless products and programs available which promise to help people lose weight. Many of these programs are unreliable at best. At worst, they can be dangerous, even fatal. Many of them have very serious side effects, many others are unreliable, and still others simply do not work. If you are trying to lose weight, it is best to get the whole story on these products before you lay down your money—and your health.

If It Sounds Too Good to Be True . . .

Have you ever watched reruns of *The Honeymooners?* Or *I Love Lucy?* Or even *Seinfeld?* There is a common theme that comes up in many classic episodes of these timeless sitcoms. Ralph and Norton, Lucy and Ethel, and Jerry, George, Elaine, and Kramer often come up with outrageous schemes that will, they are certain, make them "get rich quick." Invariably their schemes backfire. Ralph freezes up in front of the camera when making a commercial, Lucy gets drunk on the tonic she is trying to sell, and Kramer burns down the client's country home.

It is all great fun to watch. Indeed the concept of getting rich quick without risk and without work is a temptation that is very hard to resist. We can relate to the character's desire for fast, easy money. Comedy writers are well aware of this. This is why the get-rich-quick-scheme has been a comedy staple since the golden age of vaudeville. It is funny to watch people trip all over themselves, even though we know that their plan will never work. We know full well that Ralph, Lucy, and the rest will finish up the episode with only as much—or perhaps even less—money than they started out with.

Although the get-rich-quick scheme seems like a tired cliché, every year millions of people fall for similar promises about products that promise to help them "get thin quick." These products—from diet pills to herbal supplements to fat-free potato chips to exercise equipment—prey on our poor body image and on our instinct to seek rich rewards for little work.

HEALTH FOR SALE

There are so many products, programs, and services out there that it is hard to keep track of them all. What is worse, each of them makes such wonderful promises that it is very hard not to believe that if you purchase and use them, you will become thin and attractive. But there is so much more to diets, diet pills, weight-loss programs, and other get-thin-quick gimmicks than what you see on their labels and in their advertisements. Once you know the whole story, you will be able to make better and more informed decisions about them. And you may realize that you are much, much better off without them.

Diet Drugs, Herbs, and Supplements

What could be more tempting than solving your weight problem by simply taking a pill? Diet drugs come in many forms and are used by many people to curb their appetite and shed unwanted pounds. And although being overweight may pose some health risks, the risks of these drugs are often far worse than any threat posed by extra weight or even obesity.

At the Drugstore: Over-the-Counter Diet Pills

Many diet drugs are easy to get. Just walk into your local pharmacy, even your supermarket, and buy as many as you like. Readily available to people of all ages, these drugs seem safe simply because they are so easily available. After all, if they were dangerous, they wouldn't be so easy to get, right? Wrong. Products like Acutrim and Dexatrim rely mainly on a drug call phenyl-propanolamine (PPA), a dangerous stimulant. Side effects of PPA include high blood pressure, which can cause hypertension and serious heart problems. Other side effects include anxiety and paranoia, even seizures.

Of course, the law requires that the side effects

of these products be noted on the product label. However, the dangers are usually printed in super-fine print and can be difficult to understand. Many impatient consumers do not even bother trying. Instead they read only the huge, banner-sized promises of fast weight loss that are printed across the front of the box in brightly colored type.

Because these products are readily available, there is no way to determine how many individuals are consuming them. Easy to get—and seemingly harmless because of their availability—they are often abused. The dangers spelled out on the rarely read warnings are doubled and tripled by consumers who take too many or who continue to take the pills for longer than recommended.

At the Doctor's Office: Prescription Diet Drugs

People often believe that if a product comes from a doctor, it must be good for them. When a doctor prescribes a medicine, they take it without even thinking about it, Many people are so used to taking a pill for what ails them that they seek "cures" from their doctors for conditions that are not really ailments at all but basic attributes of their body. They want to lose weight so rather than changing their diet themselves, they seek a "cure" for their appetites from their doctor.

Many years ago it was common for doctors to give their patients amphetamines to help them lose weight. These pills speed up the nervous system and cause the body to burn more calories, which is how they came to be known as "speed." Amphetamines have very dangerous side effects, including heart trouble and high blood pressure.

They are also highly addictive. What is worse is that users often found themselves unable to slow down, relax, or sleep. The drugs made them anxious and nervous, and they often used other drugs, most commonly barbiturates ("downers") to help them slow down the body. This combination of uppers and downers often proved deadly. So users of amphetamines may have taken off some weight, but they often became drug addicts in the process. They may even have died from it.

One would think that with the lessons learned by doctors back then, they would be more careful when considering new diet drugs that come onto the market. But the population's desire for a miracle "fat cure" creates a constant demand for drugs that promise to help people shed pounds. And drug manufacturers know that if they can develop such a drug, they have a market ready and willing to try it out. These companies work very hard not only to produce the drugs but also to ensure that the drugs receive approval from the government's Food and Drug Administration (FDA). With heavy and very expensive lobbying in Washington, DC, these pharmaceutical companies know that they can get their products to market despite their harmful side effects.

One of the newest drugs to hit the market is Meridia. Meridia affects the appetite control centers in the brain. But it also affects the heart and can cause high blood pressure. It is only recommended for people who suffer from obesity, and it works only when used in conjunction with a diet and exercise program as prescribed by a doctor. So it is not a "miracle cure" for obesity or an easy way to shed a few pounds if you are mildly overweight. It can also be physically and emotionally addictive. When combined with other drugs—diet drugs in particular—it can be quite dangerous. And as a new drug, one can never be too sure of its long-term effects. But Meridia has been approved by the FDA and is now available with a doctor's prescription.

Other drugs have been approved by the FDA only to be taken off the market later on when their dangers became clear. A few years ago, in 1996, several new drugs were made available by prescription that promised to help people lose weight. One was Dexfenfluramine, a diet drug marketed under the name Redux. Redux worked by increasing the levels of serotonin, a naturally occurring chemical that balances a person's emotional sense of well-being. The other was a combination of fenfluramine—a weight-loss drug that had been available for many years—with phentermine, a stimulant that counteracted the side effects of the first drug, which was known to make people lethargic. The combination pill was called fen-phen, and like Redux it worked by meddling with the brain's natural levels of serotonin. Scientists believe that by increasing the levels of serotonin in the brain, the drug made people emotionally more content and helped them to lose weight.

Known side effects of Redux and fen-phen include diarrhea, fatigue, and dry mouth as well as pulmonary hypertension, an often fatal heart condition. But many people ignored these side effects or were not properly advised of them by their doctors. What is worse, many diet centers made the drugs available to their clients without the kind of medical supervision that was really needed. Users stayed on the drugs for longer than the prescribed period of time. The drugs were abused in other ways as well, by users who did not provide their doctors with complete information regarding their medical history or use of other drugs. And as time went on, more serious long-term effects became apparent, including memory loss, depression, and damage to the heart, brain, and nerves. In 1997 both drugs were taken off the market by the FDA, a very rare occurrence.

The "Health Food" Store: Herbs and Supplements
Just as people sometimes believe that anything that comes from a doctor is good for them, so too do they sometimes consider any product that is labeled "natural" or "herbal" to be a healthy choice. But nature produces plenty of natural drugs that are as dangerous as chemicals. Although many herbal remedies have proved to be just as effective as pharmaceutical ones, some herbs have proven to be detrimental to our health, even fatal.

One would think that the very nature of the health food store would guarantee that nothing you find there could possibly be bad for you. After all, doesn't it say "health food" right there on the sign? Many health food stores and "nutrition" centers sell a variety of products that claim to help people change their weight. Some of these supplements are aimed at people who are trying to lose weight. Others are aimed at people concerned with building up their bodies and adding muscle. Both kinds of supplements have serious side effects. Yet because they are not drugs, they are not subject to the scrutiny of the FDA and can be placed on the market without the warnings that are required on prescription and over-the-counter drugs. So many people purchase and use these herbs blindly, believing they are harmless and ignorant of their side effects.

St. John's Wort is an herb that affects people's moods. It has been used for many centuries as a cure for depression. In recent years it has been used by many people who are trying to lose weight. As with fen-phen and Redux, it is believed that by elevating people's moods, these drugs suppress their appetite and help them to shed pounds. St. John's Wort has several known side effects, including an extreme sensitivity to sunlight. Although that may seem minor, consider the fact that sunburns can cause cancer, and you might see it a bit differently.

A popular supplement that is supposed to help people lose weight is a combination of St. John's Wort with other herbs like ma huang (ephedra) and others that contain ephedrine. Ephedrine acts like an amphetamine, speeding up the central nervous system. And like the uppers these herbs resemble, they can be quite addictive and very dangerous. Ephedrine can increase blood pressure and has been known to cause stroke. Supplements that combine ephedrine with St. John's Wort are sometimes marketed as herbal fen-phen, because, like the banned drug, they are a combination of mood-elevating and stimulating ingredients. But most people do not consider the fact that like fen-phen they also have harmful and even fatal side effects.

When considering any herbal remedy it is important to think critically about why this product is being sold. Many people believe that everyone involved in the health food industry is a gentle hippie, seeking only to spread the word and share the wealth of what nature can provide. But in truth, herbal supplements are marketed in much the same way as pharmaceutical drugs and manufacturers are just as profit-motivated as the big drug companies. Americans spend $700 million a year on herbal remedies. But because these remedies are not drugs, they are not subject to the scrutiny of the FDA.

Muscle Potions: Dietary Supplements

Like herbs, dietary supplements do not require FDA approval. As a result, many products that have not been proven to work are available to consumers. Some people who are trying to change their bodies turn to dietary supplements that are supposed to help them put on weight. They are trying to bulk up and gain muscle while burning more fat.

One common dietary supplement is dehydroepiandrosterone, commonly known as DHEA. DHEA is supposed to slow down the aging process, help the body burn more fat, and build muscle mass while strengthening the immune system. None of these claims have been proven. In fact, prior to 1985, DHEA was an over-the-counter drug. But, since its claims could not be substantiated, it was banned by the FDA. Clever marketers repackaged the stuff as a dietary supplement, thereby avoiding the FDA's requirements.

Although the results of DHEA have never been proven, some dangerous side effects have been. High doses of DHEA can cause menstrual problems in women and like steroids may bring on masculin-ization—hair growth, lower voice, and other mascu-line traits. In men, use of DHEA can cause an enlarged prostate, even prostate cancer.

Skipping Lunch: Liquid Meals

One of the most appealing weight-loss products around is readily available and especially enticing to those who want to lose weight in a hurry without much work. Meal replacement shakes are supposed to take the place of breakfast and lunch, allowing only one lean meal per day, with snacks of only fruits and vegetables or—surprise!—a fat-free "candy" bar or pudding made by the same company.

These products are nothing new. They first appeared in the 1930s when a Chicago doctor began selling a mixture of chocolate, whole wheat, bran, and starch as "Dr. Stoll's Diet Aid, the Natural Reducing Food." Sold at beauty parlors, the product was supposed to replace breakfast and lunch, and help ladies (who bought the product at beauty par-lors) to slim down.

Today Dr. Stoll's legacy lives on in mass-marketed liquid meals like Slim-Fast and Nestle's Sweet Success. These shakes promise to provide all the nutrition of a healthy meal in a filling shake that tastes as good as what you'd get at the ice cream parlor. But the vitamins and minerals in the shake are not as good for you as they would be in a meal. And there is little chance that drinking one of these shakes will satisfy a healthy appetite. Even a real milkshake, complete with fattening ice cream, would not satisfy your hunger the way that a sand-wich or a big salad would, right?

The fact is that these diet shakes are probably worse for you than they are good. Sure, they promise to help you lose five pounds in one week, and if you stick to the program, you will see a small difference on the scale at the week's end. But the fact is that you would see the same difference if you ate a healthy, low fat meal three times a day, and you would not be as hungry. And the Slim-Fast cure is rarely a lasting one. Most people gain the weight right back as soon as they start eating normally. What is more, doctors believe that having your weight yo-yo up and down is far worse for you than being a few pounds overweight.

At the Grocery Store

The diet product industry is far more than just drugs meant to control or suppress your appetite. At every grocery store—just a few aisles away from the healthful, low-fat foods we should be eating in order to lose weight and/or maintain good health—are countless products that promise all the flavor and convenience of the snacks and junk foods we have come to rely on but with less fat and calories. From diet soda to fat-free cookies to low-fat frozen dinners, food companies are betting that the promise of low-fat will lure shoppers toward their products. And often, they're right—simply seeing the words "low-fat" on a box of cookies makes many shoppers believe that they can have the best of both worlds: that they can lose weight and still indulge in the rich, delicious cookies that they love.

Prepared Diet Meals

Ever since the 1950s, when the TV dinner was

invented, Americans have come to rely on the convenience of frozen dinners. And with our nation's obsession with losing weight, it only makes sense that many of the products in the frozen food aisle promise to be low in fat and calories to help dieters lose weight. There are many kinds of prepared diet meals on the market today. Some are only available through weight loss programs like Jenny Craig and Nutri/System. Others, like Weight Watchers and Healthy Choice are found right next to the french fries in the frozen food section of the supermarket. These products promise to deliver gourmet dinners, lunches, even breakfasts that will help dieters stay on their own programs.

But these kinds of products usually come up short on both sides of that bargain. The portions are usually quite small, leaving diners still hungry after they have eaten what was supposed to be a sensible meal. The feeling that they are not satisfied by what is considered healthy can make them feel bad about themselves, and make it harder for them to stick to their diets. And the meals which are low-fat are often loaded with salt to give them added flavor, and high sodium carries as many health risks as high-fat.

Low-Fat Snacks and Sweeteners
Have you ever noticed how there's a diet version of just about everything? Diet soda, no-calorie sweeteners, and sugar-free candy are as common as apples at the supermarket. But are they really good for you?

In nature things that are sweet are usually good for you. Nature made things like cherries, tomatoes, and oranges taste good so that people and animals would eat them and be healthy. Things that are poisonous are often bitter or sour. So our craving for sweet things is really a healthy one. And if we always reached for an apple, pear, banana, or mango whenever we felt that craving, we would all be quite healthy and probably quite slim. But nowadays we are more likely to reach for a chocolate bar, an ice cream cone, or a piece of candy. And The result is all too often a weight problem.

Artificial sweeteners, like drugs, are chemical substances. They too have side effects that can cause health problems after many years. Saccharin, for example, has been linked to some forms of cancer. Before you become a diet soda fiend or begin replacing the sixteen-calories-worth of sugar in your coffee with an artificial sweetener, think about it. You would be better off satisfying your sugar jones with something sweet and natural.

Fat-Free

Andre was trying to take off a few pounds, so he went food shopping with his dad to ensure that he would have the kinds of foods that would fit into his low-fat diet. In the cookie aisle, he found himself putting back the chocolate chip cookies that he loved so much and grabbing instead a bag of fat-free devil's foodcake cookies. That night after dinner, Andre opened the bag, hoping to satisfy his nightly craving for chocolate. He ate one cookie. It was okay, but he was still craving chocolate. Instead of the two or three chocolate chip cookies he usually ate for dessert, he found himself eating the whole bag.

There is a common misconception among dieters that products claiming to be fat-free can be eaten with reckless abandon. The fact is that fat-free products may be nonfat, but they are sweetened with lots of sugar. If you do not burn off the calories from the sugar, then your body will convert them to fat. In the end, you would have been just as well off eating the more fatty, delicious cookies.

When doctors say that a healthy diet should be low in fat, they are telling us to eat less meat and dairy and more fruits, vegetables, legumes, and whole grains. But consumers took the advice the wrong way. Doctors wanted them to replace chocolate bars with fruit, but people instead replaced them with fat-free chocolate bars that are fat-free but still high in calories and of little or no nutritional value. And they never taste as good. Essentially people deprive themselves of the foods they love for no great benefit.

Fake Fat

In 1998 a new product hit the market that promised to make fatty foods available in a fat-free form. Olestra, a fat substitute made from sugar and soybean oil, was approved by the FDA in 1996. Olestra mocks the flavor and consistency of fat, but its molecules are too big for the body to digest, so it is simply passed through the digestive tract without being absorbed. This means that you can indulge in the greasy-tasting potato chips you love, and the fat will simply pass through your body.

Sounds great, right? Well, maybe. It is true that foods made with Olestra taste very much like their fatty counterparts. And it is true that they will not make you fat the way regular chips can. But there is a price to be paid just the same. Because Olestra is not digested by the body, it runs right through you, working like a laxative. It can bring on serious cramping, loose stools, and severe diarrhea. Not so pleasant, huh? What is worse, it can carry lots of vital nutrients right out of your body along with all the fat. Olestra hinders the absorption of carotenoids, the anti-oxidants so important in preventing cancer. It also prevents your body from absorbing fat-soluble vitamins (A, D, E, and K). So although it is preventing you from absorbing fat, it is also robbing you of nutrition.

WEIGHT-LOSS AND DIET PROGRAMS

Many people who want to lose weight do not know where to start. For guidance, they turn to everything from weight-loss centers to support groups to books to articles in supermarket tabloids.

Weight-Loss Programs

There are hundreds of thousands of weight-loss centers in the United States today. One of the oldest and most successful programs is Weight Watchers. Weight Watchers is focused on teaching people to control their portions and learn good eating habits. Joining the group involves attending weekly meetings, at which members are weighed and discuss their dieting troubles. Weight Watchers has its own line of prepared foods, but the program is not dependent on it. Members can easily keep track of their calories and fat while eating everyday foods. Many members enjoy the familial atmosphere of the club and take comfort in the support of the group. However, Weight Watchers can be intimidating for self-conscious dieters who do not wish to talk about their diet dilemmas in front of the group. Some members also might find it hard to keep track of their meals and calculate their daily intake of fats, carbohydrates, and so on, which can make sticking to the plan difficult. It can also become quite costly. Members are required to pay a weekly fee, and the program's prepared meals—if one decides to use them—can be expensive. However, once members have reached their goal weight, they can continue to come to meetings and take part in the program for free, which can be beneficial to keeping the weight off.

A second kind of weight-loss program is tied more closely to strict dietary guidelines. These programs, including Nutri/System and Jenny Craig, require that members eat only the foods prepared by and for the program. These prepared meals, which can run from fifty to one hundred dollars per week, leave members with limited choices and large expenses. Although following these diets can result in fast and noticeable weight loss, keeping the weight off is difficult. One cannot eat prepackaged food forever.

In addition to counseling and diet planning, many diet centers now offer herbal supplements in addition to their other services and products. These products are, again, questionable in their effectiveness and are potentially harmful.

Fads

Fad diets have been around for decades. Like the liquid lunch plans, these diets promise to help you get thin quickly by following a strict regimen, often replacing regular meals with low-fat, low-calorie substitutions. Sometimes they give meal plans for several weeks, claiming that chemical reactions in certain foods will help you lose weight. These diets, sold in books like *The Zone, The Scarsdale Diet, Dr. Atkins Diet Revolution,* and other best-selling books promise to provide guidance in planning meals and cutting fat and calories. They range from high-protein diets to liquid diets to bizarre fasts that require dieters to eat nothing but grapefruit, broth, or Jell-O.

Cutting the Carbs: High-Protein Diets

One of the strangest and most popular trends in diets these days is diets that eliminate all carbohydrates and increase the intake of protein. Essentially this means cutting out all bread, fruit, vegetables, and sugars and eating only meat and dairy products. This reversal of the food pyramid sounds bad for you—and it pretty much is. Yet the books that promote these diets—*The Zone, The Carbohydrate Addict's Diet,* and *Dr. Atkins' Diet Revolution*—have sold millions of copies.

These diets do seem to take weight off quickly. But the weight loss is due more to water loss and the fact that low-carb means low calorie. Losing all those vegetables and grains means losing important nutrients, including not only vitamins and minerals, but also cancer-preventing fiber. What is worse, more meat and dairy means that your body is also getting more cholesterol and fat and that your kidneys will have to work overtime to get rid of all the nitrogen in meat, which can cause damage. Most doctors will not recommend these diets. In fact, in the fall of 1997 they were denounced by the American Dietetic Association, the American College of Sports Medicine, the Women's Sports Foundation, and the Cooper Institute for Aerobics Research.

Grapefruit, Cabbage, and Other Wacky Diets

Every so often someone announces that a particular food contains some kind of miracle ingredient that will help people shed pounds. The grapefruit diet and its modern equivalent, the cabbage diet, require eating hardly anything other than these ingredients for two to three weeks.

In the short term these diets do work. And why wouldn't they? By eating nothing but cabbage stew or grapefruit for fourteen to twenty-one days, you are essentially starving yourself. The grapefruit diet, for example, provides less than eight hundred calories per day, hardly enough to keep the body functioning for long. In the long term most dieters who try these programs—all of which are recommended for only a few weeks—gain the weight back soon after going off the diet. Those who stay on the diet endanger their health. If you continue to eat according to these plans beyond the set time limits, you could develop—and may already have—an eating disorder.

EXERCISE PROGRAMS AND PRODUCTS

Edna wanted desperately to get into shape. She had seen an advertisement on television for a machine that promised to help her trim her *waist in just minutes a day. For $79.99 she could have this piece of simple equipment right in her bedroom. She ordered the Crunchmaster and eagerly awaited its arrival.*

When it finally came, Edna was startled. This pile of pipes and pads bore little resemblance to the rolling bars that she had seen movie stars working with on television. When she finally got the thing put together, she watched the instructional video that showed how to use it. With her head on the padded neck support and her hands gripped tightly around the handles, she attempted to do her first crunch. She couldn't move. She kept slipping and couldn't complete the rep. She tried for a good ten minutes and finally gave up, feeling ridiculous. She tried one or two other nights but never quite got it. The contraption was put down in her basement where it gathered dust and rust. Although the product was guaranteed, she never bothered to return it to get her money back.

Of course the only way to really get in shape is to eat a healthy diet and get the right amount of exercise. Once upon a time most people had to walk to school and to work. Most jobs involved manual labor, and those that didn't left enough time for healthy activities like bicycling and swimming. But today people drive or ride everywhere. Our economy is such that there are few manual labor jobs around anymore. Most of us work behind a desk. Students are not expected to go work the fields of the family farm after class. Yet most of us still eat a high-fat diet similar to that of our great-grandparents. This is a main reason why so many of us are overweight.

So it goes to follow that people are constantly seeking ways to get some exercise in the little time we have. Since we cannot walk to places we need to go, we now spend time walking nowhere on a treadmill. Since we cannot go skiing too often, we buy expensive cross-country skiing simulators. Since we do not need to do manual labor to earn a living, we spend our free hours lifting weights.

Gyms and Health Clubs

One way to get exercise is to join a gym or health club. Members of these clubs pay a monthly or annual fee to gain access to the gym's equipment and/or to take exercise classes. Memberships are very expensive, costing anywhere from several hundred to several thousand dollars per year. Often these membership fees do not include the services of a personal trainer, without whom it might be difficult to create a safe and effective workout routine.

While gyms and health clubs are no doubt beneficial, they do not do the work for you. Working out, be it with weights, on machines, or in aerobics classes, is just that—*working.* When you start, you may be unable to perform well. You may be out of breath quite quickly on the stepper, or you might find yourself unable to bench press anything at all. It can be frustrating, and since gyms are fairly public places, some people find themselves embarrassed. Many people who join gyms with visions of a buff new body stop going not too long after they start. What is worse, they are often committed to pay for the membership for a full year, which means they continue to pay even after they have stopped going.

If you choose to join a gym or a health club, be sure to keep these setbacks in mind, be patient, and do your best without overdoing it.

Home Gym Equipment

Some people think that by purchasing exercise equipment for their home, they can have the benefit of a gym without having to leave their home or do anything in public. These products range from a few simple dumbbells to thirty-dollar gimmicks to expensive, gym-quality cardio machines that can run upwards of a thousand dollars.

If you choose to buy your own equipment, think carefully about your needs. Some smaller machines work your muscles for a little while, but if you do it regularly, you will quickly outgrow the resistance and get no further benefit. Expensive machines can take up an entire room, and many of them will perform only one kind of exercise or work only one muscle group. With exercise, as with diet, it is important to diversify. Only buy what you intend to use and use what you buy. Some people make using their home gym a habit. Others wind up with a very expensive and unattractive coat rack.

UNDER THE KNIFE: COSMETIC SURGERY

Plastic surgery has been around for many years and has helped countless people who were born with defects, burned in fires, disfigured in accidents, or who lost breasts to cancer. But today many people—young and old, men and women—

are opting for elective cosmetic surgery. Doctors surgically remove fat from their bodies through liposuction. Some men have had their muscles augmented surgically, and women have had their breasts either reduced or enlarged. Although cosmetic surgery was once performed primarily on women, the number of such surgeries performed on men is rising steadily.

Many teens think about cosmetic surgery as a way to alter their bodies. But there are many complexities, even dangers, associated with these surgeries. Teens' bodies are still growing, and the effects of cosmetic surgery over a lifetime can be unpredictable. There are so many other possibilities for altering your body and looking good. So much can be improved simply through healthy diet and moderate exercise. Why take the risk?

4
What Are Eating Disorders?

*T*eena, Jennifer, and Kristie were quite a threesome. Juniors in high school, they had been a tight clique since elementary school. All three girls were very thin—painfully thin.

Back in the seventh grade, they began to notice that their bodies were changing. Kristie was getting a little pudgy. Jennifer's hips were getting a bit wide. Thin Teena's parents were both heavy, and she feared a similar fate. The three girls began dieting together, slowly at first, just making a vow to keep themselves away from candy and ice cream. Soon, they were counting calories, measuring waistlines, weighing in nightly on their bathroom scales. Pounds dropped off all three youngsters. Dieting became a game at first, but then it developed into a full-scale war against fat.

Eating barely two meals a day, Teena cut out all meat and dairy products, telling her parents that she was a vegetarian and would

72

eat only vegetables. Unlike true vegetarians, she supplemented her diet with no soy products, beans, or other nutrient-rich foods. When she sat down to dinner with her parents, she ate only salads of iceberg lettuce and carrots and dishes of rice and mushrooms. Occasionally when her hunger became too strong, she would add some salad dressing and bread. At fifteen, five-foot-three-inch Teena weighed only ninety pounds.

Kristie had more of a struggle to maintain her rail-thin figure. When she could not shed pounds as fast as Teena, she found herself stocking up on over-the-counter diet pills and diet shakes. Her appetite suppressed by the diet pills, she was able to sit down to a meal and eat very little, moving food around the plate and passing some down to the dog, tricking her parents into thinking that she had eaten more. She longed to be as thin as Teena, but even though she was three inches taller, she felt that at 100 pounds she was overweight.

Jennifer made it seem the easiest. While the other girls sat at lunch staring hatefully at their diet shakes or salads, Jennifer indulged in a sandwich, a soda, even some cookies. It was easy, she claimed, to get rid of the food through the use of laxatives or by simply throwing up.

We need food to live. Eating can be one of life's pleasures, providing not only nutrition that we need to survive, but also satisfaction and enjoyment and a reason to gather with family and friends in an important daily ritual. But for many women and men dieting has become a way of life. What happens when dieting becomes an obsession, when food becomes the absolute enemy?

For many young women and some young men, losing weight is an endless battle. They diet, exercise, abuse diet drugs and weight-loss products, even starve themselves in order to become more slim. Often they see themselves as being overweight even though they have little or even no body fat. Their self-image is so skewed that even though they may appear emaciated to everyone else, when they look in the mirror, they see someone who is simply too fat.

ABOUT EATING DISORDERS

Eating disorders are not your average diseases. They are not caused by germs, viruses, or bacteria. They arise in response to deep-seated emotions. They are influenced by the thoughts and the acts of those around us and by society at large. They are serious, and unfortunately common, psychological disorders. They are related to body image and to self-esteem, and they can affect and be affected by conditions like depression.

Eating disorders are obsessive disorders. People who suffer from them are unable to stop or control their self-destructive behavior on their own. They need medical attention to be well. And without medical attention these disorders can quickly turn deadly. In 1983 alone 103 deaths in the United States were directly attributed to anorexia. Many others may have been caused by complication arising from such eating disorders.

The reasons why some people get disorders are diverse and complicated. Social, biological, and psychological factors all play a role. The constant bombardment of media and personal messages regarding body image, our society's unhealthy pre-occupation with food and weight, and family relationships all play a role.

As many as 8 million Americans suffer from eating disorders according to the National Association of Anorexia and Associated Disorders (ANAD). About 90 percent of those diagnosed with eating disorders are women. For the relatively small population of boys and men who suffer from problems like anorexia and bulimia, the disorder is further complicated by the assumption that they are "women's problems." But even among women many eating and related disorders go unnoticed. Anorexics often hide their thinness by wearing loose, baggy clothing. Bulimics usually binge and purge in secret. People who suffer from compulsive eating disorders are often dismissed as merely having no self-control rather than as suffering from a serious medical problem.

COMMON PROBLEMS

Eating disorders are not new. They are a common—and growing—problem. Many celebrities have struggled with eating disorders including Diana, Princess of Wales, Geri "Ginger Spice" Halliwell, singer/songwriter Fiona Apple, feminist author Naomi Wolf, actress and fitness guru Jane Fonda, and 1970s pop singer Karen Carpenter whose death brought attention to the problem.

But eating disorders are conquerable. Just ask Kate Dillon, a fashion model who gave up a lucrative career as a "straight size"—that is, underweight—model to get healthy. She once weighed in at only 120 pounds, which is pretty darned thin when you are nearly six feet tall. She was, at the time, a bona-fide anorexic. But now she is skinny no more. Comfortable in a size sixteen, the 165-pound beauty takes pride in her size and continues to make a fine living as a plus-size model. What is more, she is happy and healthy.

Other women in the spotlight have fought similar battles. Fiona Apple was widely criticized for her waifish figure until she revealed that she was well aware of her own battle with food, which stemmed from a violent rape at the age of twelve. And the Princess of Wales, whose struggle stemmed from her unhappy marriage, seemed to be on the road to recovery at the time of her tragic death in an automobile accident.

ANOREXIA NERVOSA

The food on Christina's plate was all wrong. How could she eat steak on a Tuesday? How could she eat steak at all with all that fat? And potatoes, mashed with butter and milk? What was her mother thinking?

Quietly she moved a few things around on her plate and nibbled on a few spears of broccoli. Tomorrow, she thought, I will tell mom I'm becoming a vegetarian. No more meat. No more dairy. Just peas, and broccoli, and asparagus. And fruit. Lots of fruit. I will be healthy. I will be thin. And I will not have to worry about steak on Tuesdays anymore.

Anorexia nervosa is one of the most deadly psychological disorders known today. Although many problems of the mind have a direct effect on the body, none of them have as profound an impact as anorexia. People with this disorder do not eat enough food to be healthy. They are malnourished, and in many cases they are starving themselves to death.

Anorexia usually begins in the teens, but according to the FDA, incidences of the disorder among eight- to eleven-year-olds are increasing. It can occur in a relatively short episode—a dramatic weight loss followed by recovery, all within a couple of months—or it can be a chronic, long term condition that continues for years. Like drug addicts, anorexics often make recoveries only to find that they relapse later. In addition to dieting, anorexics may engage in compulsive exercise or purging to lose weight, further compromising their health.

But the symptoms—and the causes—of anorexia go far beyond diet, weight, and body image. Anorexia is often rooted in or triggered by emotional trauma or other psychological conditions. Anorexics are not simply unhappy with their bodies—they are unhappy with themselves or with their lives, and they express their inner distress by focusing on their food, their weight, and their bodies. Their relationship with food becomes distorted. They begin compulsively counting fat and calories. Eventually, like Christina, they assign other often arbitrary requirements to their meals.

Wasting Away

But it doesn't end with what they eat. An anorexic's problem often revolves around the fat on her body. She will see herself as overweight even when it is obvious to everyone around her that she is too thin. She will usually drop about 15 percent of her body weight. Malnourished, her body will stop menstruating. Her breasts will shrink. In a pubescent anorexic they will not develop. In extreme cases her organs may be adversely affected. Damage to the heart and kidneys is common. Many anorexics (about 5 percent) die from the disorder. Most common in girls aged thirteen to seventeen, anorexia also occurs in grown women as well as in boys and men.

Often anorexics are considered overachievers. They excel at sports or in academic skills or social graces. Many anorexics have never been overweight by any definition. Their need to change their bodies stems more from personal issues of control than from anything else. The anorexic takes great pride in her control over the food that she eats. Her love of this control is so strong that it overshadows her own perception of herself. The anorexic is a person in denial. She denies that she is too thin. She denies that she is hungry. She denies that she is unhealthy. She thinks of herself as completely in control of her food, but in truth, she is a slave to her diet. When she looks in the mirror, she doesn't see that she has lost weight, only that she has some weight to lose. In her battle with food, she has really lost. She's become a slave to her obsession.

Although this problem is most common among

females, it can also occur in men and boys. Anywhere from 5 to 10 percent of anorexics are men. Because it is less common in men, they are more likely to go undiagnosed and untreated.

Anorexia Warning Signs

The symptoms of anorexia can range from weird little habits around the dinner table to such unmistakable evidence of malnutrition as protruding ribs and sunken cheeks. Yet taken alone, even the most obvious clues can be mistaken as symptoms of something else—fatigue or physical illness, for example—and many anorexics take special care to cover up the signs of their disorder. But the traits common to anorexics are many, and most people who suffer from the disorder will display more than one symptom. There are a number of recognized behaviors and physical signs that may indicate anorexia:

- ⊙ **An intense, obsessive fear of gaining weight.** These days, that seems pretty common, and it is. An anorexic will allow this fear to take control, even though she thinks she is the one who is in control.

- ⊙ **A sharply distorted body image.** An anorexic will perceive herself as being overweight, even though she may be underweight—even emaciated. She will continue to lose weight but will never be satisfied that she is thin, no matter how thin she becomes.

⊙ **Weight stays the same when it should be increasing.** During adolescence when the body is growing, it should be getting heavier. Many young anorexics deprive themselves of the nutrition needed to grow, and so their weight remains the same when it should be increasing as a normal part of growth.

⊙ **A preoccupation with food and weight.** An anorexic will diligently count calories and fat and will usually note her weight on the scale once or more per day.

⊙ **A noticeable or severe weight loss.** Anorexics will shed pounds very quickly. A loss of 15 percent of one's body weight is considered the red flag, a sure sign of an eating disorder.

⊙ **Very poor self-esteem.** This symptom can be very hard to recognize because many anorexics are overachievers who do well in school, sports, and other endeavors. The fact that they are not happy or confident is often obscured by their high level of achievement.

⊙ **Covering up with loose or baggy clothes**. One would think that if someone lost 15 percent of her body weight—say, went from 115 pounds to 98 pounds—there is no way anyone who knows her would be able to miss it.

But anorexics often wear loose, baggy clothing that makes them appear heavier than they are. They do this not only to escape notice from parents who would undoubtedly become concerned by their thinness but also because the anorexic still feels that her body is fat and unattractive and wishes to cover it up.

⊙ **The body starts making concessions.** It is not natural for people to be too thin, and when people starve themselves, the body reacts in particular ways. It starts by slowing down—even stopping—particular bodily functions. That is why women who grow too thin will cease to menstruate. Blood pressure will also fall, the breathing rate will slow, and young anorexics will stop growing.

⊙ **Hair, nail, and skin reactions.** Skin, hair, and nails will become dry and brittle as body weight decreases. Soft hair will begin to grow all over the body to keep it warm as fat decreases.

⊙ **Weird or compulsive eating habits.** Anorexics revel in their mastery over food. Sometimes this is expressed not only in their control of how much they eat but also in how they eat it. They often develop bizarre requirements for their meals. *I will not eat anything that* *cannot be eaten with a spoon. I will not let the fork ever touch my lips. I will eat only foods that are green and red, but I will not eat green and red food together. I will eat only fruit.* These habits—and many of the other symptoms of anorexia—are also common among people who suffer from another common eating disorder, bulimia nervosa.

BULIMIA NERVOSA

Anita couldn't believe she'd done it again. But she had been so depressed over the B she got on an English exam, she had gone and done it without thinking. But of course, she had known all along that she would do it again. After all, that is why she kept the box of Ring-Dings in the closet. She had gone through all of them in about five minutes and then went down to the kitchen and finished off a quart of milk, seven peanut butter and jelly sandwiches, a jar of pickles, and a pint of ice cream. And then, of course, she had gone diligently into her mother's bathroom, rested her arms on the cool porcelain of the toilet, and vomited until she couldn't throw up anymore.

For the bulimic food is both a trusted friend and a bitter enemy. Similar to anorexia, bulimia is a common psychological disorder that centers around an unhealthy attitude towards food and body image. But an anorexic will continually deny herself basic sustenance. By contrast, a bulimic will habitually indulge in large quantities of fattening foods and then get rid of them by vomiting or through the use of laxatives. Bulimics may purge only occasionally—when they are upset or nervous—or regularly. Some bulimics report that they have binged and purged as often as twenty times per day.

This cycle of bingeing and purging wreaks havoc on physical as well as emotional health. Many bulimics, like Anita, use food as both a reward and a punishment. Their connection to food is highly emotional and can cause dramatic mood swings. Their need to act impulsively with food can influence other areas of their lives. Many bulimics have been known to shoplift, speed, or engage in other impulsive, high-risk behavior. They are also very likely to suffer from depression, even to consider suicide.

Bulimia and Anorexia: What's the Difference?

Anorexia and bulimia are both eating disorders, and they are very similar in terms of the people they affect and the ways in which they are manifested. They share many symptoms and causes, and they both have severe physical and emotional consequences. Both anorexics and bulimics have an abnormal preoccupation with food, weight, and body image. Often a person who suffers from one of these disorders will suffer from the other at another point in their lives. About half of the people who suffer from bulimia have battled with anorexia at some point, and many anorexics have some symptoms of bulimia. Pop singer Karen Carpenter, for example, suffered from anorexia. She not only starved herself but also used Ipecac syrup to induce vomiting and purge food from her body. The long-term buildup of the highly toxic drug eventually caused her heart to stop.

But there are some key differences between the two disorders. Whereas an anorexic will deny or fail to recognize her own problem, a bulimic is usually quite aware of her disorder and will go to great lengths to keep it a secret. A bulimic will usually not lose weight in the dramatic way that an anorexic will. Bulimics can be of normal weight or slightly over- or underweight.

Although bulimics and anorexics share many symptoms—a fear of gaining weight, an obsession with food, a need to be thin—there are a few key symptoms that are more likely to indicate bulimia.

Signs and Symptoms of Bulimia

Bulimia usually begins in conjunction with an effort to lose weight. But the cycle of bingeing and purging can quickly spin out of control. Bulimia most often develops in women in their teens or early twenties, but because bulimics keep their problem a secret, they usually do not seek treatment until they are in their late thirties or forties.

The symptoms of bulimia range from vague to explicit. Although the disorder is usually kept a secret, there are some signs that are almost impossible to ignore.

◉ **Bingeing.** A binge involves downing anywhere from 3,000 to as much as 10,000 calories in about a an hour—keep in mind that the average woman consumes from 2,000 to 3,000 calories per day—and is the hallmark of bulimia. Bingeing is usually done in a secret place and is rarely detected by friends and family.

◉ **Purging.** Some bulimics can make themselves throw up by simply thinking about it or by sticking their fingers down their throats. But others often abuse products like Ipecac syrup—a product used to induce vomiting after the ingestion of poison—to help them get rid of food. Some bulimics will also use over-the-counter laxatives or even enemas to induce bowel movements and get rid of their food that way. Bulimics will go to great lengths to keep the process a secret, often running the shower so that nobody will hear them purge.

◉ **Hoarding.** Bulimics will often hide a secret stash of favorite binge foods—like Anita's emergency crate of Ring-Dings—to have them available when the need to binge strikes.

◉ **A severe emotional connection to food.** Bulimics use food to deal with their feelings. If they are depressed, unhappy, afraid, tense, or nervous, they may be overwhelmed with the need to overeat and then purge.

⊙ **Mood swings.** The reliance on food to deal with difficult feelings creates a vicious cycle. A bulimic eats because he or she is depressed, then purges, and then may become elated or more depressed.

⊙ **Physical signs.** Vomiting is a natural reflex that the body relies on to get rid of poisons, sour foods, and bad bacteria. But it is not something the body is equipped to do often, and the process of constant purging causes some specific physical symptoms. Blood vessels in the face will break, causing obvious red lines in the skin. Hands, feet, and face can become swollen. Acid from the stomach can cause rapid tooth decay and gum disease. Less obvious are some of the other ways that bulimia takes its toll on the body: weak eyesight, damage to the kidneys, heart, and bones, and the potentially deadly erosion of the esophagus and stomach lining.

COMPULSIVE EATING DISORDER

Eddie was never happy with his weight. He had been teased since he was a little boy and had never been successful in his attempts to lose weight. He was unhappy with the way he looked and every time a diet failed, he would console himself with food. A big meal became his best friend. If he was angry, he would stop at the drive-through on the way home from work and order four cheeseburgers, two orders of fries, and a milkshake. If he was upset, he would go out to dinner at a fancy restaurant and order the richest, most indulgent dish on the menu. When he was lonely, he would stay home and finish off a few pints of cookie-dough ice cream. On some nights he just ate whatever he could find—pickles, peanuts, corn chips, tacos, leftover stew, or a loaf of bread. He would just eat until he fell asleep.

Compulsive eaters respond to stress by eating. Like bulimics, they have developed an unhealthy emotional relationship with food and will often binge when they are in states of severe depression, stress, or anger. But unlike bulimics, compulsive eaters do not follow up their binges with bouts of purging. What is worse, many compulsive eaters typically do not get enough exercise. Sometimes they don't get any at all. As a result, most compulsive eaters are over-weight, even obese. Their lives—and their bodies—are dominated by thoughts of food.

Compulsive eating disorders—like other eating disorders—are usually rooted in psychological trauma or emotional unhappiness. Eddie, for exam-ple, turned to food when he needed to quiet emo-tions of sadness, fear, and loneliness. Many compulsive eaters feel unloved and unwanted, and finding no satisfaction in these parts of their lives, turn to the temporary satisfaction that a full belly gives them as a substitute. The process becomes addictive, and the person comes to depend on food to provide the satisfaction that they cannot find elsewhere in their lives. Although everyone overeats occasionally, compulsive overeaters do it often. Their desire to overeat begins to overwhelm every aspect of their lives.

The health risks of compulsive overeating can be serious. Usually compulsive overeaters are overweight, even obese, and they rarely get the exercise they need. The foods they crave are often loaded with sugar, fat, and salt and can bring on such illnesses as heart disease and diabetes. The added weight can aggravate chronic illnesses like asthma and put pressure on the joints. What is worse is that many chronic overeaters may fight an unending battle with their weight, losing weight only to put it back on soon after. This kind of "yo-yo dieting" has proven to cause more harm than good, and most people would be better off maintaining a steady weight even if they are somewhat overweight.

But by far the worst repercussions of chronic overeating are the emotional ones. In a society that values slimness and control over fat as well as active lifestyles, those who appear to have no self-control and who do not exercise regularly are maligned. Chronic overeaters feel tremendous guilt after a binge, which can lead to depression or further bingeing episodes.

EXERCISE ADDICTION

Angelo got up every morning at 5 AM and ran

seven miles before heading out to school. After school it was off to the gym, where he would spend forty minutes on the stair climber, followed by a complete circuit of the weight machines, and then another forty minutes in the free-weight room. Three times a week he took karate, and two nights a week he took a stretching class. And if he didn't spend a half hour on sit-ups, push-ups, and pull-ups each night, he couldn't get to sleep.

Can someone be addicted to exercise? Well, seeing as when we exercise, our bodies release endorphins—natural stimulants that provide a natural "high"—it makes sense that people can become as addicted to exercise as they can to cigarettes, alcohol, or cocaine. And they do. But exercise addiction is related to more than just that natural high. It is usually rooted in a deep-seated fear of fat, and for that reason, it is often discussed in the context of eating disorders.

Exercise, like eating, is a natural behavior. It is something that should be good for people, and in fact most Americans do not get enough of it. But for some people the need to be thin and active overrides good health, and exercise can become dangerous. Many people begin to use excessive exercise as a tool for getting rid of fat in much the same way that bulimics use vomiting or anorexics use dieting. In fact, some anorexics and bulimics use exercise to "get rid" of food after a meal or binge. People who are addicted to exercise might count the calories that they burn in much the way that an anorexic might count the calories they consume. They are constantly battling with their bodies, trying to get them to work harder and burn more and more fat.

Like anorexics, compulsive exercisers can find that their body weight falls dangerously below normal. This means that the body burns so many calories exercising that it does not have enough nutrients to support basic bodily functions, like fighting a cold or menstruating. Factor in the excessive strain on the heart, lungs, and other organs that continuous exercise causes, and you've got a recipe for serious illness, including heart failure.

The same stimuli that lead some people to disordered eating lead others to take the potentially beneficial activity of exercise to a dangerous extreme. They see constant and ever-increasing exercise as a method for ridding their bodies of unwanted fat as well as increasing their muscle tone, strength, and endurance. Even when they have a strong, muscular physique, they may see themselves as fat or, in some cases, may see themselves as lazy or lethargic whenever they are not exercising.

In our fitness-crazed society, it is little wonder that many people are exercising to excess. If we are not as active, as muscular, as toned, as strong, or as slim as the people we see on television or in magazines, we might get the impression that we are lazy and worthless. After all we are constantly being told that fat is bad, that all we have to do is buy some sneakers and "do it" to win a perfect body and perfect health. These messages combine with the same ones that affect our body image in regard to food. People might exercise to excess believing that by being more active and fit, they are better people.

SEEKING TREATMENT

Eating disorders pose very serious health risks and should be treated with extreme caution. If you or someone you know seems to be suffering from a problem with food or weight, there are recovery methods and programs that can provide help. It is imperative that anyone who has experienced a dramatic weight loss get medical attention immediately.

Most eating disorders require two kinds of treatment, medical and psychiatric. The short- and long-term effects of disorders like bulimia and anorexia can be deadly, and medical attention is needed to make sure that the body does not entirely shut down. Many people with advanced cases of anorexia or bulimia have to be hospitalized. They may have to be tube-fed to keep their bodies going.

But the emotional aspects of eating disorders can be harder to diagnose and to treat. Many anorexics are in complete denial of their problem and will lie about their diet and their feelings while continuing to believe that they are fat. Some might eat just enough to be considered "cured" and then go back to their diets as soon as the coast looks clear. Like a person battling alcoholism or drug addiction, those who suffer from eating disorders face a long and difficult battle, first to recognize their problem and then to deal with it and make themselves healthy again—both physically and emotionally.

TYPES OF TREATMENT

Jake stared at the ceiling. He had been in the hospital for four days with a tube in his arm sending vital nutrition into his system. He was ashamed to be there and wondered how it had happened. "I don't have anorexia," he thought to himself. "I'm just not hungry."

Jake had started dieting the year before, when he was worried about making his weight for a wrestling meet. A two-day fast had gotten him down to the proper weight, and he realized that denying himself food could be a powerful tool. He enjoyed the feeling he got when he skipped a meal, the control it gave him. Only he could decide what he ate—not his father, not his coach, not his teammates, just him—and he began doing it more and more often. Ten months later, and more than twenty pounds lighter, Jake had not gone to a wrestling meet since the previous school year. "But I don't have anorexia," he told himself again. "Only girls get anorexia."

There are many kinds of eating disorders, and the reasons why people get them are as diverse as the people who suffer from them. There is no one easy cure that will put an end to everyone's problems with food and weight. For someone like Jake, whose weight has fallen too far, treatment might begin with a stay in a hospital, attached to feeding tubes. But where does it go from there?

There are many options ranging from psychoanalysis and therapy to twelve-step programs. Someone like Jake might benefit from group therapy to show him that yes, boys do get eating disorders. Or perhaps he would benefit from a self-help group that would help him to gain power over his problem and might appeal to his need for control.

The important thing is to realize that recovering from an eating disorder means not only healing your body—gaining (or losing) weight, learning to eat in a healthy way, and counteracting the damage that the eating disorder has wreaked on your body—but also healing your mind. Therapy is key to understanding how and why an eating disorder has developed and learning how to develop a healthy attitude toward food, your body, and your life.

Most eating disorder sufferers in treatment will have to meet with a therapist—either a psychiatrist, psychologist, social worker, or other expert—to discuss their problem. Their doctor may prescribe certain drugs like Prozac that will treat any depression that might accompany the eating disorder and have been shown to be especially helpful to people who are suffering from bulimia or binge eating. In addition they will probably require that the individual take part in some form of group therapy. By talking with and listening to other people suffering from the same disorder, many people come to realize that they are not alone and that they can learn to love their bodies and be healthy.

But the road to recovery is often a rocky one. Most eating disorder sufferers are never really "cured." They must fight their urges to binge or deny themselves food for the rest of their lives. For this reason many support groups have developed to offer comfort and support to people who suffer from eating disorders. Groups like Overeaters Anonymous apply the same twelve steps that made Alcoholics Anonymous so successful to people who are powerless over food. Similar groups exist for people who suffer from anorexia and bulimia as well as exercise disorders. And online communities have sprung up that offer information, chat, and newsgroups for people with any of these kinds of problems.

DO YOU HAVE AN EATING OR EXERCISE DISORDER?

- Do you think that you are fat even though friends and family have told you that the opposite is true?

- Have you recently lost weight amounting to 10 to 15 percent of your pre-diet weight?

- Do you ever refuse to eat even when you are very hungry?

- Are you terribly afraid of gaining weight?

- Do you ever consume large amounts of food in excess of 1,000 calories in a single sitting?

- Do you exercise immediately after eating in hope of burning all the calories you have consumed?

⊙ Do you ever use ipecac syrup or your fingers to induce vomiting after eating?

⊙ Do you ever use laxatives or enemas to stimulate bowel movements after eating?

⊙ Do you hoard food?

If you have answered yes to any of the questions above, you may have an eating disorder and should seek help immediately.

5 Depression

Michael just could not get out of bed. In his room with the shades drawn tight, he lay in the dark, unable to sleep but somehow not able to get up either. He felt hungry all the time but was unable to eat. He was sad but didn't know why. He hated school and faked sickness often—or simply cut class—in order to stay home. He no longer felt comfortable in his own body. He quit the football team and no longer ran track. Put simply, Michael hated himself and hated his life. He found no comfort in his friends, and he was unable to relate to his family. He felt depressed and painfully alone.

Everybody gets a bit down in the dumps once in a while. It is quite normal to have some days when you just can't imagine getting up, going to school, and dealing with the sometimes traumatic and tumultuous activity of your everyday life. But for some people that feeling comes far too often and stays far too long. For them the normal challenges of daily life can become too much to handle. Their fears, apprehensions, and lack of enthusiasm grow from a passing mood to an overburdening sense of despair. Like Michael they cannot see past themselves. They are depressed, and they may require help.

CHANGES AND CHALLENGES

Part of growing up is going through many emotional and physical changes. Teens are regularly faced with tremendous pressure to "fit in" and may worry more about what their friends think than they will at any other point in their lives. You have probably been going through some changes lately, and perhaps have had some trouble adjusting to your new body and your new role as a young adult. You may have heard your parents tell you, "It's just a rite of passage." But the stress and struggles of the teen years can be very difficult.

The normal changes of your teen years—growth spurts, menstruation and breast development in girls, growth of body hair, increased perspiration—are made even more difficult by the completely new social situations and personal feelings that arise as we grow from children to adults. Unfamiliar sexual curiosity and interest, shift in friendships from same sex to mixed groups, concern about your future, and planning for college or a job may make you excited and frightened at the same time. You may suddenly find that you identify more with your friends than you do with your family and that your desire to fit in with your peers may cause some conflicts with both your parents' values and your own need to establish yourself as an individual. You may find yourself wanting to rebel against adult authority while you conform to the norms of your own generation.

Looking at this list, you have a lot to handle. You are in the midst of very turbulent times indeed, and although the emotional roller coaster is considered "normal," there is a darker side to it that is not, marked by rebellion from authority, sometimes substance use and abuse, and sexual promiscuity. Most of the time, however, you should feel happy, be physically active, and have some positive relationships in your life. If you are sad, lonely, and angry most of the time, you may be depressed.

WHAT IS DEPRESSION?

The National Institute of Mental Health defines depressive illnesses as illnesses that affect mood, body, behavior, and mind. Depressive disorders are not the normal ups and downs of life that everyone experiences. They are marked by extreme bouts of sadness, loneliness, and despair, and perhaps most important, they often have a physical component. There is no simple cause for depression—no virus, parasite, or singular occurrence or exposure that brings it on. It is caused by a combination of factors including life changes, emotional distress, and—importantly—a chemical imbalance in the brain.

In addition to outside influences, depressive disorders are caused by neurological troubles. The chemical messengers in the brain are not giving the right instructions. Things have kind of slowed down in the nervous system, and this slowdown has harsh effects on the way a person feels both physically and emotionally. There is some evidence that depressive disorders, or at least a tendency toward them, may be genetic. This means that depression can run in families. If your mom or dad has ever been depressed, you may be at risk for depression as well.

Your initial thought may be that a depressed person is very quiet, calm, and isolated like Michael in the story that opens this chapter. But this is not always the case. Among teens in particular, depression may be marked by increased anger and frequent confrontation with parents and others. It is not always the quiet person locked away in his room that is depressed. Perhaps it is that friend who is always trying so hard to rebel—dressing in black clothes, listening to Marilyn Manson, and lashing angrily against her parents, teachers, the police, and society at large. Or it may be your classmate who struggles so hard to fit in or be "perfect"—the girl who studies into the night in order to bring home straight As, or the boy who diligently practices on his jump shot at every possible moment.

Depression is not an uncommon problem among adolescents. Anywhere from 4 to 8 percent of teenagers—or one out of every five teens—is depressed. Sadly most of them will never seek or get treatment. Depression is different than other illnesses because it is hard to understand. When children are depressed, parents may feel defensive, afraid that their child's unhappiness is a reflection of their own parenting skills. They may refuse to acknowledge their child's condition, brushing his or her behavior aside as merely a phase. But depression is a real danger to teens and can lead to self-destructive behavior including drug and alcohol abuse, self-mutilation, risky sexual behavior, even suicide.

DEGREES OF DEPRESSION

Tony had just been denied the scholarship he wanted. He had studied all year and gotten straight As, and his SAT scores were great. He just didn't have enough extra-curricular activities. Although Tony was sure he would be able to gain admittance into any number of colleges, the lack of scholarship funds meant that he would have to narrow down his college choices quite a bit—boarding at a private university was no longer really an option. He told his parents that he wasn't upset, but they noticed that he seemed to be very quiet for a few days. He stayed in his room and did not wish to go out with his friends on the weekend. They were a little concerned, but after three days Tony told them he would like to take a trip to visit one of the state universities that had a program he was very interested it. He seemed to have come to terms with his dilemma, and was beginning to look at solutions.

Depression comes in many shapes and sizes from inexplicable bouts of "the blues" to short "downers" brought on by bad news to more severe depressions that last for months or even years. Mental health professionals diagnose mental disorders in categories by the symptoms each patient reports. Depression can range from mild with only a few symptoms to severe with a person losing the ability to be safe and independent. The degree of a person's depression will determine the type of treatment needed.

Tony in the story above is going through a minor depression brought on by some bad news. When you experience a loss—be it the death of a loved one, a friend moving away, the ending of a romance, or the loss of an opportunity such as the one Tony went through—depression is a natural phase that most people go through on their way to acceptance. The good news is that Tony has gotten through the phase and is beginning to emerge from his depression on his own.

For the past two weeks Amy has been withdrawn from family and friends. She is not hungry and feels as though there is a big knot in her stomach. Despite all her mother's efforts, she just can't bring herself to eat. Amy feels very sad and upset because of a breakup with her first boyfriend, Todd, whom she had dated for five months. He now is dating another girl, and Amy feels hurt and angry. Her friends tell her that he is a loser, but she cannot stop thinking about him, all the fun they had together and this promise to take her to his junior prom. Now she can't go. Amy is tearful, unable to sleep, and tired at school. She can't concentrate. She feels she will never meet someone like Todd again. Amy's friends and family are very worried about her. She tries to listen to them, but her heart is aching.

Amy is depressed. Her sleep and eating are disturbed, her schoolwork is beginning to be affected, and she feels hopeless. But she is only mildly depressed. The good thing is that she is still allowing her friends and family to support her during her crisis. Having someone to talk to is very important. Someone like Amy might benefit from counseling to help her through her crisis.

Ben had been an honor student and involved with many after school activities. He was goalie on the soccer team, he served on student government, and he worked at the school radio station. Ben's parents are in the process of divorce, and for the past six weeks Ben has begun to change. Ben is cutting school and, instead of his old soccer buddies, has been hanging around with the "burnout" crowd at school. He has begun smoking marijuana and rarely takes a shower. Ben has gained ten pounds from overeating and is angry all the time.

Ben lives with his mom, and she started dating another man three months ago. Ben lets her know he does not like this. He sleeps all day and goes out all night with his new friends. He won't listen to either of his parents or to his old friends who have tried to reach out to him. Ben was just arrested after throwing a bottle through another driver's window whom he says cut him off. He told the arresting officer, "I just don't care anymore. Nothing really matters, does it? You can all go to hell!"

Ben is severely depressed. He has pushed away all of the positive influences in his life and is going in a negative direction. He is not dealing with his feelings and is giving up on himself and others. Ben is in need of professional help and is in danger of spiraling further downward.

SIGNS OF DEPRESSION

Depression can manifest itself in many ways. It affects not only a person's mood but often his or her appearance, performance at school or work, and behavior toward others. There are a number of signs and behaviors that might indicate a depressive disorder.

- ⊙ **Poor performance in school or at work.** If a person becomes suddenly disinterested in things that once challenged and excited him or her, it may be a sign of depression. Such a change in attitude is most often seen in teens in the form of falling grades.

- ⊙ **Withdrawal from friends and activities.** A depressed person may find social situations painful and will often want to be alone even though he or she is lonely.

⊙ **Lack of enthusiasm or motivation.** Similarly a depressed person might find it impossible to get excited about upcoming events or to think about the future.

⊙ **Sadness and hopelessness.** Many depressed people find themselves unable to look ahead, to see past their own depressed state of mind. They act sad all the time and may cry often.

⊙ **Anger and rage.** Other depressed people might react to their situation not by retreating to their loneliness but by lashing out at those around them.

⊙**Overreaction to criticism.** A depressed person may be extremely self-critical. Fits of anger, bouts of crying, and extreme defensiveness are common reactions to criticism from anyone else.

⊙ **Poor self-esteem.** Depression can make people painfully self-aware. Depressed people can be harshly judgmental of themselves and often exhibit behaviors linked to poor self-esteem.

⊙ **Indecision, lack of concentration, or**

forgetfulness. These kinds of problems can affect more than just schoolwork—they can affect one's ability to drive, read, or even enjoy a movie.

⊙ **Restlessness and agitation.** Unhappy with themselves, depressed people may develop a feeling that the thing that will make them happy is just out of their reach. They may feel a need to go chasing after elusive dreams or become frustrated with their lives as they are.

⊙ **Changes in eating or sleep patterns.** Any serious change—inability to sleep at night or a sudden inability to get out of bed in the daytime may be indicative of depression.

⊙ **Substance abuse/alcohol abuse.** Depression is often accompanied by substance abuse because the depressed person turns to drugs or alcohol to quiet their emotional pain. These drugs may bring on a feeling of calm for a short while, but they usually make depression even worse.

⊙ **Poor hygiene.** Depressed people will often "give up" on themselves, and this is often expressed through a lack of attention to personal hygiene. They might avoid showering, haircuts, shaving, or all of these things.

◉ **Thoughts of death or suicide.** When a person expresses a fascination with death or a desire to end his or her own life, it is a certain sign of depression and should be taken very seriously. Anyone with suicidal thoughts should receive clinical help immediately.

GETTING HELP

Andre's sisters were very worried. He had always been a very moody guy, either excited or extremely down in the dumps. But this summer it seemed to be getting even worse. He stayed up all night reading or just sitting in the dark with his bedroom door shut. Then he slept all day. He did not go out with his friends and didn't bother to get a summer job, saying that there was nothing he needed to spend money on. He rarely showered or shaved, and he wore the same sweatpants all the time. He looked horrible, and he smelled most of the time.

When his three sisters expressed their concern to their mother, she shrugged them off. "He's just a bit eccentric," she said. When they continued to pester her, she replied, "What can I do? Take him to a doctor? He's not sick. That's just the way he is."

Because depression is a disease that is for the

most part psychological, it often goes untreated. Parents who would rush their child off to the doctor at the first sign of a cold, who regularly give their sons and daughters drugs to fight off ear infections and strep throat, will often ignore the fact that their child is depressed and that there is help available.

Parents may have a hard time recognizing depression because of their own fears. They might feel that their children's psychological trouble will reflect badly on them as parents or that they somehow might have caused it. They are afraid that they have failed their children. In other cases, they are simply too far removed from the trials of young adulthood to remember just how traumatic the teenage years can be. And finally there is a tendency among most people—parents and other family included—to dismiss the symptoms of depression as being brought on by the person exhibiting them. "He acts that way because he wants to." "She likes to wallow in self-pity."

Unlike a virus or a broken bone, depression is not an easily understood sickness. There is no simple cause-and-effect reasoning behind depression and no simple way to cure it. Consider the story about Andre and his three sisters. His sisters sense that something is wrong, but his mother thinks it is just his personality. She cannot fathom how—or why—medical attention might help her son.

Steps to Helping a Child or Friend

Depressed people are caught in a cycle of depression and often cannot find their own way out. By looking out for friends or family members, you do their homework for them and can help them get the treatment they so very much need. Follow these steps to help out a loved one whom you think might be depressed.

- ⊙ Monitor his or her mood and behaviors over time, taking note of the severity and frequency of mood swings and behavior changes.

- ⊙ Listen to the person and offer hope and help.

- ⊙ Invite and encourage the person to participate in activities he or she once enjoyed.

- ⊙ Educate yourself about depression and the resources available.

- ⊙ Consult a mental health professional about your concerns and get advice on how to address the depressed person.

- ⊙ Sit down with your friend and tell him or her why you are concerned. *"Dawn, over the past few weeks I have noticed you have been so sad and withdrawn—I am very worried about you. You seem like you may need some help."*

- ⊙ Explain that you have found an agency or a doctor that might be able to help, and that you hope he or she will call.

⊙ Offer to make the appointment for the person if he or she does not feel up to it.

⊙ Do whatever it takes to get him or her to the appointment. Offer to go with the person. Try to empower your friend; avoid making punitive gestures or comments—he or she feels bad enough already.

⊙ Accompany your friend to the appointment and agree to participate if requested.

⊙ Continue to be supportive and empathetic.

⊙ If your first attempt to help fails—try again.

⊙ Encourage the person to stick with the treatment plan, including medications if prescribed.

TREATMENTS FOR DEPRESSION

The truth is that there are many effective treatments available for depression. They range from simple changes in diet and lifestyle to therapy and drug treatments. For example, a great many people suffer from what is known as Seasonal Affective Disorder (SAD). During the winter months, when the days are shorter and they spend most of the daylight hours indoors, these people become terribly depressed. It has been proved that this is because they do not get enough sunshine. So doctors have developed special lights that mimic the rays of the sun. Sitting in front of these lights for a period of time each day has proven to be an effective treatment for this kind of depression. More severe forms of depression have more complex treatments.

If you think that you are depressed, the most important thing to do is get help without delay. The longer you wait, the worse you will feel and the more risky your situation may become. Talking to your family doctor about how you have been feeling is important so that any medical causes for your symptoms can be evaluated. A good physical exam should help your doctor evaluate your physical health. Blood tests may be done, and the doctor may ask you to share some of your feelings with him or her. The doctor may suggest you seek counseling or therapy, or she may prescribe a medication to help in conjunction with therapy or refer you to a psychiatrist for medication.

Therapy

Angie states, "I had been feeling really down for four months and started therapy with our school psychologist, Ms. Kelly, two months ago. You see, I had been very upset because I could not improve my SAT scores, despite constant drilling and a very expensive preparation course. I felt as though I was letting down my father, and I felt stupid around my two best friends, both of whom scored almost 100 points higher than I did. I am ranked tenth in the school, and I want to go to Princeton, like my dad did.

It really helps having someone outside my family and friends to talk to about my fears and struggles. Ms. Kelly and I have been talking about all the pressure I have been under and the impact this stress has made on me. I know now why I have gained ten pounds, cannot concentrate, and have withdrawn from my dearest friends. We have also met with my dad who told me how proud he is of me and how it doesn't matter what school I go to as long as I am happy. It turns out that he has been worried but did not know what to say because I would get so upset any time he tried to talk to me. And I did. Now I am starting to set more realistic goals for myself and hope that I can continue to feel better.

Counseling and therapy is the first line of treatment for depression. It is important to find a therapist with whom you are comfortable because you will have to talk about the very personal emotions that you are experiencing. Your therapist must provide complete confidentiality so that you can talk candidly about what is happening at home, school, and with your friends. If you have someone to talk to, the burdens may not feel as heavy, and you may not feel alone with your problems. Ms. Kelly utilized both individual and family therapy to help Angie deal with her depression. In therapy all of a person's psychosocial issues will be assessed. This includes drug and alcohol use as well as family dynamics, which may be the reason someone is depressed.

There are many mental health agencies or professionals offering therapy for depression. You may see a social worker, psychologist, or a psychiatrist. You will spend time talking alone with your therapist, and you may also work in groups with your family or with other people who are suffering from the same kind of depression. During your therapy sessions, you will discuss and try to come to terms with family problems, significant losses in your life, your perception of yourself, and your self-esteem. You will learn to set realistic goals, build positive relationships, and set comfortable boundaries. You will also work on establishing a new, positive routine and on pursuing activities that will help you feel happy and healthy.

Medication

Medication is commonly prescribed for depression because we know that the chemicals in the brain may not be working right. Only a psychiatrist can prescribe medications, so if you are seeing a therapist who is not a medical doctor, he or she may have to refer you to a psychiatrist who will determine if you are a good candidate for prescription antidepressants like Zoloft, Paxil, and Prozac. They are referred to as Selective Serotonin Reuptake Inhibitors (SSRIs). They work by altering the level of serotonin in the brain. (Recall that serotonin is a chemical that exists naturally in the brain and balances a person's sense of well-being.) It is very important to understand that these are not quick-fix pills. They usually must be taken for anywhere from four to six weeks before they begin to have any kind of an effect. But once they do, they can help to fix the imbalance in your brain that is causing your depression. Like any drug, these medications can have some side effects so they must be taken carefully; similarly, they must not be abused. And they are not a one-stop cure. Antidepressants are prescribed in conjunction with therapy.

Hospitalization

In cases of severe depression, doctors may suggest or require that a patient be hospitalized in order to receive round-the-clock treatment, support, and attention. Hospitalization is a rather serious measure, most often used when depression has put someone's personal safety at risk—when the person is in danger of hurting himself or herself or others, or when the patient is suicidal.

With the safety of the patient as the top priority, specially trained teams work with the patient. In the hospital, a depressed patient can expect to receive individual and group therapy as well as treatment with antidepressants. More serious treatments, including electroconvulsive therapy—commonly known as shock treatment or ECT—are sometimes prescribed for adults and and have proven helpful in some very severe cases of depression. However, such treatments—which can have very harsh side effects—are not recommended for adolescents. Hospitalization, therefore, is most often used to provide severely depressed adolescents with care, therapy, and treatment, and to ensure that they do not act out in dangerous ways.

While adults may determine on their own that they require hospitalization, adolescents cannot sign themselves in for this kind of treatment. Young people may be hospitalized through a doctor's recommendation, and a parent or legal guardian must consent to the treatment. In some instances, a judge may order inpatient psychiatric hospitalization because an individual is considered to be a danger to him- or herself or others. This is somewhat rare but it does occur, especially if the teen is suicidal.

Because hospitalization seems like a dramatic step, many people are resistant to it. However, hospitalization is able to provide what other forms of treatment cannot: giving depressed teens an opportunity to stay in a safe space with constant attention while their illness is treated.

ARE YOU DEPRESSED?

Maybe you think some of the feelings of depression described in this book apply to you, but you're not sure if you are depressed. Consider the way you have felt or behaved over the past two weeks and then answer each of these statements with either "true" or "false."

⊙ I have felt sad and/or irritable.

⊙ I am often angry with my friends or family.

- I have overreacted to criticism or been tearful or outraged for little reason.

- I lack interest or pleasure in activities that I used to enjoy.

- I prefer to stay home alone all day and have been cutting school to do it.

- I have stopped hanging out with my closest friends.

- I am not doing as well in school as I once did.

- There has been a dramatic change in my appetite. I have gone on eating binges or not eaten at all for long stretches of time.

- I have had trouble sleeping or have been sleeping all the time.

- I have felt excessively guilty about something I did or did not do.

- I have had difficulty concentrating on my schoolwork and other responsibilities, and/or I have difficulty making decisions.

- I have been forgetful or unable to remember things I used to recall easily.

- I am tired all the time.

- I feel as though nobody likes or cares about me.

- I feel that things are terrible and that

they cannot get any better.

⊙ I have thought about hurting myself or
   ending my life.

According to the National Mental Health
Association, if you have answered "true" to five or
more of the above questions, you may be
depressed and should seek help.

6 Preventing Suicide

*T*iffany is sixteen, and she lives with her parents and older brother in northern California. Tiffany has always been a little wild and taken risks. She has always hung around with kids a bit older than she and experimented with drugs. In the three months since she got her driver's license, she has gotten two speeding tickets, prompting her parents to take her car keys away. She has been preoccupied with death since she was thirteen but now has become even more infatuated with it. In her school notebooks there are drawings of the grim reaper, men jumping from bridges, and bloody knives.

Tiffany is very angry at her parents for selling the family home and planning to move to Seattle at the end of the summer. Telling her parents that she' would rather die than leave her hometown, she has taken to spending more and more time away from her family.

Her drug experimentation has escalated from smoking joints to snorting heroin. She barely speaks to anyone at home, sometimes simply coming and going to change clothes in the middle of the night. She is difficult to talk to. One day, however, she tells her older brother of this great plan she and two friends have to go to Golden Gate Park and inject as much heroin as they can get their hands on for the ultimate high—DEATH. Her brother is stunned and tries to talk to her. Again she refuses to listen. He quickly tells his parents who now act and sign her into detox and a suicide prevention program. She is safe—for now.

While it is perfectly normal to feel depressed sometimes, when sad feelings become self-destructive we are in trouble. Suicide among teenagers is on the rise in our society. In fact, there has been an increase of more than 200 percent since 1982 according to the American Academy of Child and Adolescent Psychiatry. It is the third leading cause of death for young people ages fifteen to twenty-four.

As you can see from the story about Tiffany, some of the symptoms of suicide are the same as those found in depression. Depression is closely related to suicide; in fact, the risk of suicide among people with depression is 30 times higher than it is among the non-depressed population. People who are depressed who also drink alcohol—which is by definition a depressant drug—are at an even greater risk for suicide. Other psychological disorders may also increase the risk of suicide. A recent study at the University of Minnesota School of Public Health indicates that teens who habitually binge and purge—the key symptom of bulimia nervosa—are more than four times more likely to attempt suicide than teens who don't. Among chronically depressed people, suicide can be difficult to foresee because once depressed people make a decision to end their lives, the depression may seem to lift. They might appear more healthy than they have in years, when in truth they have to end their lives.

SUICIDE SIGNALS

The most important time to act on someone's behalf is when the depression leads to suicidal thoughts. After a suicide many survivors are left to look at the now deceased loved one's behavior and wonder how they missed the signs. These signs are very clear, and if people know how to recognize them before it is too late, many suicides might be prevented.

- ⊙ **Giving away personal possessions.** Suicidal people will often prepare for their intended deaths by giving their prized possessions to their friends and loved ones. An unexpected gift of a favorite sweater or book could be their way of secretly saying good-bye to you.

- ⊙ **A suicide plan.** If someone talks about

suicide, and he or she has a precise plan, he or she is probably quite serious. You should take this seriously. Talk to your friend about it and get help for him or her.

⊙ **Preoccupation with death.** What may seem like a harmless fascination with the dark songs of Ozzy Osborne, the tragedies of William Shakespeare, or the life of Sylvia Plath might actually indicate an unhealthy preoccupation with death and suicide. Although many great works of literary art make reference to suicide (Osborne's song "Suicide Solution," or Shakespeare's *Romeo and Juliet,* for example), an unnatural obsession with these themes might indicate a desire to emulate them. A suicidal person might also express their own desires artistically, in poems, drawings, or songs that they create.

⊙ **Dramatic personality changes.** A severe desire to change who we are can be a marker for suicide. Suicidal people might attempt to reinvent themselves. A studious teen may become a slacker; a gregarious one might become shy; a sweet person may become suddenly obnoxious, or vice versa.

⊙ **Changes in appearance.** Again, suicidal teens may try to reinvent themselves, especially in terms of their looks. A very feminine girl may begin to wear baggy, boyish clothing. An average-looking boy may suddenly come home with his eyebrow pierced.

⊙ **Irrational, bizarre behavior.** Inexplicable actions—ranging from eating at odd times of day to suddenly painting one's room a freakish shade of bright red—can be indicative of depression and suicide.

⊙ **Overwhelming sense of guilt, shame.** People who plan to kill themselves may have feelings of guilt about it and express them in odd ways. In addition to giving away prized possessions, they may make apologies for unrelated, often forgotten things they have done in the past. They may find it hard to look their loved ones in the eye.

⊙ **Change in eating or sleeping patterns.** Much as in depression, changes in day-to-day life-sustaining activities can indicate a suicidal pattern.

⊙ **Family or personal crisis.** Tragedies—including divorce, remarriage, a broken romance, or a death in the family—can spark suicidal thoughts.

- ⊙ **Recent rejection or failure.** A failure to win at a sport, a spurned invitation to the prom, or a poor grade on a college entry exam are among the many disappointments that might lead to thoughts of suicide.

- ⊙ **Firearm in the home.** Studies show that the very presence of a gun can spur suicidal thoughts, and people with access to firearms are more likely to take their own lives.

- ⊙ **Incarceration.** Prisoners have a higher likelihood of suicide than the general population.

- ⊙ **Family history of suicide.** The suicide of a family member—even a grandparent when one has never met—can loom over a family for generations. People who have been raised in its shadow are more likely to turn to suicide when they are feeling hopeless.

- ⊙ **Exposure to suicidal behaviors of others.** When we hear of suicides in our schools, our towns, or even on the news, we are shaken. For severely depressed people, it may seem to offer a way out, and "copycat" suicides are not unusual.

When You Think There's Trouble

Maggie did not know what to do. Her cousin and close friend Justin had been a bit down in the dumps for a while. His father had died of lung cancer the year before, and Justin had had a hard time coping. Things got worse this spring when he found out that he had missed out on a football scholarship, his only chance at college and his father's dream for him. But Maggie had no idea of how bad it was until today when Justin gave her his football letter jacket and told her that he wanted her to have it because she wouldn't be seeing him anymore.

"Why?" she asked. "Are you moving?" He simply shook his head. When she pressed on, he finally told her that he was tired and lonely and that he was going to take his father's pistol into the woods that weekend and put himself out of his own misery. "It's not that I really want to die," he told her quietly. "It's just that I can't bear the thought of living anymore." He gave her a kiss on the cheek and went home. In a state of panic, Maggie called her mother who immediately called the police, and her sister, Justin's mom, to make sure that the gun was removed from the house.

If you think that someone you know might be in danger of suicide, it is your responsibility to get help for him or her. If someone you know exhibits some or many of the signs discussed above, you must do something. But the signs are not always as blunt as the ones Maggie got from Justin. Often they are subtle hints—a vague reference, an unexpected gift. If you suspect that a friend might be close to the edge, you need to get that person some help. Don't be afraid to get help of your own. Talk to a teacher, a parent, a guidance counselor, or a counselor at a suicide hotline about your concern. In addition you should talk to the suicidal person yourself.

- ⊙ **Trust your instincts.** Don't dismiss your concern. You could be right, and if you are, he could kill himself.

- ⊙ **Take comments and threats seriously.** When a person tells a friend that she wants to kill herself, she is asking for help. Don't act as if she is joking.

- ⊙ **Ask if he has a specific plan.** A specific plan is a red light—this person is seriously considering suicide. If he has a plan, get him someplace where he will not be able to go through with it and seek help immediately.

- ⊙ **Get help.** Talk to a parent, teacher, or even call the police. You need to make the person safe, and you may not be able to do it on your own.

- ⊙ **Try not to leave the person alone.** Suicide is a solitary act, and as long as you are with her, she is safe.

- ⊙ **Encourage him to seek help.** Get him the numbers of your local suicide hotlines, a counselor, or therapist in your area. Tell him that if he doesn't call on his own, you will arrange it for him. This is not the time to keep secrets.

Living Healthy, Living Happy

*S*eventeen-year-old Olivia was a bit over-weight, sure, but that never stopped her. She was a first-stringer on the basketball team, and she always looked great. She had a brilliant smile, beautiful skin, and a curvaceous body that all the boys noticed. Confident, smart, and pretty, she considered herself a "large" person but never used the word "fat." She took pleasure in the fact that she filled up her jeans a bit more than some of the waifishly thin girls at her school, that she was a force to contend with on the court, and that despite the teasing she dealt with as an overweight child, she was one of the most popular girls in school.

Olivia appears to be a very happy, confident young lady. That might come as a surprise to some people. After all she is, by her own admission, "large," and she does not fit the standard of beauty to which most teenager girls aspire. Yet she takes pleasure in her body and feels no shame for the twenty pounds that classify her as overweight.

We all want to be happy. Just about everything we do—studies, work, or play—are directly or indirectly related to our happiness. We need food and shelter to survive, but we need much more than that to be happy. Sometimes we grow confused about just what will bring us contentment. As our society and our lives become more and more complex, our confusion grows as well. Will more money make us happy? A new car? A perfect body? A bowl of ice cream? A winning record in track?

The simple truth is that happiness is something that comes from inside of us. We cannot buy it, but we can find it, and we can make it. Happiness comes from dealing with the pressures in our lives in healthy and positive ways. It also comes from accepting ourselves and, to a certain degree, our circumstances, and learning to improve what we have. Olivia, for example, uses her size to her advantage in sports, and she knows that her big presence and curvy body get her attention from boys.

But the pressures of adolescence go far beyond physical expectations and demands. As we grow and change on the outside, with new adult bodies, urges, pressures, and responsibilities—we struggle with change on the inside as well. We might find ourselves second-guessing every decision we make and every aspect of what makes us who we are. *Am I too thin? Am I too fat? Am I lazy? Stupid? Am I smart, or am I a geek? Do I look foolish when I dance? When I walk? Do people like me? Do the people I like like me? For that matter, do I like myself?*

This kind of self-examination is natural, but we must stop ourselves before our own self-criticism becomes detrimental to our well being. We need to look at who we are and accept ourselves, recognize our faults, and figure out how to work with them and around them.

WAYS TO STAY POSITIVE

Charles sometimes just couldn't figure out what to do. At sixteen he was starting to feel that Kevin, his best friend since the third grade, just annoyed the heck out of him. When they went to a party last weekend, it came to a head. A friend of Charles' offered them a toke off of a joint. Before Charles even had a chance to shake his head and say, "No thanks, man," Kevin piped up with "Cool, sure" and snatched the joint out of the guy's hand. Charles knew that Kevin had never smoked pot before and was more than a bit disappointed to see him jump in so quickly. Charles didn't smoke that night, but Kevin got completely stoned, later telling Charles that he was a wuss for not trying it. Charles shrugged it off, but it made him angry and depressed. He wondered how things would go between Kevin and him as they got older.

There are many healthy and positive ways to deal with the struggles of adolescence and the pressures that can begin to weigh down on you during your teenage years. The National Mental Health Association suggests that you try the following when you feel depressed, pressured, or otherwise unhappy.

Try to make new friends. Healthy relationships are central to feeling good about yourself and provide an important social outlet. During this time in your life it is natural that you and your childhood friends may begin to grow apart and begin new friendships with others. Charles and Kevin, for example, found themselves with very different ideas about smoking pot, and Charles already has doubts about the future of their friendship. Find new friends who share in your burgeoning adult interests and share the values you would like to carry into adulthood.

Keep busy. Participation in sports, school activities, or hobbies can help teens focus on positive activities rather than negative feelings or behaviors. Any activity—from singing in the choir to an afterschool job—will keep you active and help you to avoid sitting around, watching television twenty-four hours a day.

Find a support group. Anything from a church youth group to a self-help group to help you cope with a specific problem can give you the strength that comes in numbers. Facing depression, an eating disorder, or any other problem is easier when you are able to share your thoughts, feelings, and fears with people who are going through the same thing.

Ask a trusted adult for help. When problems are too much to handle, ask for help. Even if they cannot help you themselves, a parent, a friend's parent, a teacher, even your family doctor will be able to direct you towards help better than anyone your own age will.

DEALING WITH TRAUMA

Fifteen-year-old Thomas was like an explosion waiting to happen. His father's alcoholism and his mother's temper had made his life a horror for a long time, but recently it had gotten worse. After several separations, they were still together, making Thomas, his two brothers, and each other miserable. He wished that they would just divorce and get it over with. He was tired of the fighting, the anger, and the teasing quiet periods that invariably followed their making up. But he never told them this. He never told anyone about it. The neighbors, who undoubtedly heard his parents' angry screams, pretended that they didn't. And his parents—in the midst of fights— simply pretended that nothing was wrong when they were around the kids. So Thomas played their game right along with them. He never spoke to them, to his brothers, or to anyone else about the battlefield that was their home.

Many teens, like Thomas, bottle up their anger, fear, and sadness rather than dealing with them in a constructive and healthy way. They go through life pretending that everything is fine, when in fact this is very far from the truth. Thomas' anger will probably find a way to express itself somewhere. He may take it out on other kids at school or on his brothers. He may eventually find himself lashing out at his parents, or he may wind up angry at himself. What he needs to do is talk about it. If he cannot talk to his parents, he might find help in an objective party, someone outside his family. A teacher, counselor, or clergyman may help him deal with his anger and frustration.

There are many ways that we can deal with trauma. Some people pour their pain into art. They paint, write songs or poetry, dance, or sing. These can be a healthy outlet for pain and anger. As we have discussed, dark, angry art is a good indicator of inner turmoil. But in truth we cannot deal with our pain on our own. We need help. This help can come in the form of a friend who lets us cry on his shoulder, a loving parent, or an understanding teacher. It may also come in the form of a doctor or therapist. If we are clinically depressed, help might also come in the form of medication.

GOOD HEALTH

Elliot felt tired all the time. He was not sure why. Depressed? Or just unmotivated? Uncertain, he mentioned it to his family doctor when he went in for a regular check up. The doctor took a few blood tests to check for diseases, and he ran a few tests on his muscles and reflexes. He asked him questions to determine if he was depressed. He also asked Elliot how he spent most of his time, what did he do on weekends and after school. Elliot revealed that he was an internet freak and liked to surf the Web, play games, and participate in chat rooms. The doctor told Elliot, "I'll run the tests just in case, but I think what you really need is a bit of healthy outdoor activity. Get out in the sunshine for a few hours after school each day. Really. Take a long walk each afternoon for a week or two, and see if you feel any differently."

We are plagued by messages about our health. *Don't smoke. Eat your vegetables. Get plenty of exercise.* These messages—which often come from government or nonprofit sources—are often contradicted by the commercial messages that we receive from profit-minded corporations that tell us that being healthy does not mean eating more whole foods and incorporating moderate exercise into our lifestyles but instead depends on striving for almost impossible goals of weight and body type.

The truth is that there is no one single body type that can be used as a standard for everyone. "Healthy" and "skinny" are not one and the same. Further a healthy body comes not from dieting but from proper nutrition. It comes not from constant exercise but from an active lifestyle, possibly incorporating a healthy exercise regimen but often meaning more moderate measures—simply walking to school, perhaps, instead of riding the bus.

If you struggle with your weight, the best place to start is with your family doctor. He or she will be able to calculate what your healthy weight should be and determine if you are actually overweight or underweight. If you are, you may be referred to a nutritionist who will assess your diet and help you to modify it sensibly. Similarly a doctor will make sensible recommendations about the amount of exercise you should be getting.

However, it is important to remember that being overweight does not mean that you are in poor health. Even though for many years we have been told by the healthcare industry that some of the biggest killers in our society—among them heart disease, high blood pressure, and stroke—could be prevented by a low-fat diet, recent studies indicate that in many cases, constant, failed attempts to lose weight may be more detrimental to our health than simply being overweight. As stated in *The New England Journal of Medicine,* "We should remember that the cure for obesity may be worse than the condition." If you are overweight but engage in a healthy, active lifestyle, you are probably better off simply continuing as you are than you would be fighting an endless battle of the bulge. Losing weight only to gain it back through yo-yo dieting not only puts an unnecessary and unhealthy strain on your body, but it also wreaks havoc on your self-esteem and can lead to depression and eating disorders.

Glossary

anorexia nervosa   An eating disorder in which one intentionally starves oneself.

binge   To consume large amounts of food, often in secret and usually without control.

body image   A person's opinion of him- or herself based on attitudes about his or her body.

bulimia nervosa   An eating disorder in which a person eats normal or large amounts of food and then rids the body of the food by forcing oneself to vomit, abusing laxatives or diuretics, taking enemas, or exercising obsessively.

calorie   A unit to measure the energy-producing value of food.

compulsive eating disorder   An eating disorder marked by uncontrollable eating of large amounts of food.

cosmetic surgery   the process of altering one's appearance through a surgical procedure.

denial   Refusing to admit or face the truth or reality of a situation.

depression   A state of extreme and prolonged sadness.

Glossary

diet   a method of trying to lose weight by restricting calorie intake; often contributes to the onset of an eating disorder.

diet drugs   Drugs that are supposed to aid weight loss by increasing the body's metabolism or by suppressing the appetite.

inpatient   A patient who is treated and remains in a hospital or a clinic for treatment.

internalize   To keep problems or emotions bottled up inside yourself.

obsessive   Excessive to the point of being unreasonable.

outpatient   A patient in a clinic or hospital who does not live in the hospital but visits on a regular basis for treatment.

overachiever   A person who strives for success beyond what is expected.

psychiatrist   A doctor who is trained to treat people with mental, emotional, or behavioral disorders.

self-esteem   Confidence or satisfaction in oneself; self-respect.

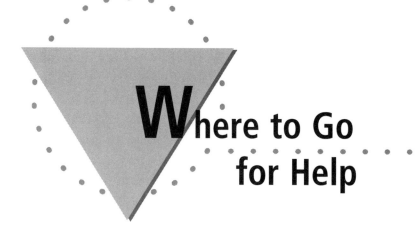

Where to Go for Help

Organizations

American Academy for Child and Adolescent
  Psychiatry
3615 Wisconsin Avenue NW
Washington, DC 20016
(800) 333-7636

American Anorexia/Bulimia Association, Inc.
165 W. 46th Street, Suite 1108
New York, NY 10036
(212) 575-6200

Center for Eating Disorders
7601 Osler Drive
Towson, MD 21204
(410) 427-2100

Depression Awareness, Recognition and
    Treatment (D/ART) Program
National Institute of Mental Health
6001 Executive Blvd. Room 8184 MSC 9663
Bethesda, MD 20892
(800) 421-4211

National Association of Anorexia and
    Associated Disorders
P.O. Box 7
Highland Park, IL 60035
(847) 831-3438

National Mental Health Association
1021 Prince Street
Alexandria, VA 22314
(800) 969-NMHA

Web Sites

About Face Body Image Facts
http://www.about-face.org

Depression Awareness, Recognition and
    Treatment (DART) Program
http://www.nimh.nih.gov

Healthy Weight Journal
http://www.healthyweight.org

Mayo Clinic's Health Oasis
http://www.mayohealth.org
National Mental Health Association
http://www.nmha.org

U.S. Food and Drug Administration
http://www.fda.gov

For Further Reading

Barrett, CeCe. *The Dangers of Diet Drugs and Other Weight-Loss Products.* New York: Rosen Publishing Group, 1999.

Bennett, Cherie. *Life in the Fat Lane.* New York: Delacorte, 1998.

Burby, Liza N. *Bulimia Nervosa: The Secret Cycle of Bingeing and Purging.* New York: Rosen Publishing Group, 1998.

Garland, E. Jane. *Depression Is the Pits, but I'm Getting Better: A Guide for Adolescents.* Washington, D.C.: American Psychological Association, 1998.

Gelman, Amy. *Coping with Depression.* New York: Rosen Publishing Group, 2000.

Hesse-Biber, Sharlene. *Am I Thin Enough Yet? The Cult of Thinness and the Commercialization of Identity.* New York: Oxford University Press, 1997.

Hornbacher, Marya. *Wasted: A Memoir of Anorexia and Bulimia.* New York: HarperCollins Publishers, 1998.

Kolodny, Nancy. *When Food's a Foe: How to Confront and Conquer Your Eating Disorder* (rev. ed). Boston: Little, Brown & Co., 1992.

Levenkron, Steven. *The Best Little Girl in the World.* New York: Warner Books, 1981.

McCoy, Kathy, and Charles Wibblesman, MD. *Life Happens: A Teenager's Guide to Friends, Failure, Sexuality, Love . . .* New York: Berkeley, 1996.

Moe, Barbara. *Inside Eating Disorder Support Groups.* New York: Rosen Publishing Group, 1998.

Smith, Erica. *Anorexia Nervosa: When Food Is the Enemy.* New York: Rosen Publishing Group, 1999.

Index

A

adolescence, 8
   physical changes of,
      8–10, 14, 91, 119
   psychological changes of,
      10–11, 91–92, 119
advertising, 2, 19–20, 22,
      40–41, 44–46, 69, 84
Alcoholics Anonymous
      (AA), 88
American Academy of
      Child and Adolescent
      Psychiatry, 111
amphetamines, 47–48
anger, 15, 96, 110, 122
anorexia nervosa, 33, 34,
      36, 70–73, 126
   dangers of, 71, 72, 75
   warning signs of, 73–76
antidepressants, 87,
      105–106
Apple, Fiona, 70
artificial sweeteners, 55–56

B

barbiturates, 48
binge and purge, 34, 77,
      78, 112
bingeing, 79, 81
body myth, 19
body image, 1–2, 124, 126
   assessment of, 37–38
   emotions and, 3, 6–7,
      35–37
   health and, 6–7, 38
   negative, 2–3, 20, 25–27,
      32–33, 35–37, 68
bulimia nervosa, 34, 36,
      76–78, 126
   dangers of, 77, 80
   warning signs of, 78–80

C

cabbage diet, 61
The Carbohydrate Addict's
      Diet, 80
carotenoids, 58

Carpenter, Karen, 69, 78
compulsive eating disorder, 13, 80–82, 126
cosmetic surgery, 34, 64–65, 126

D
dehydroepiandrosterone (DHEA), 52–53
denial, 30, 126
depression, 3, 13, 36–37, 90–91, 92–97, 101–102, 127
  causes of, 16–17, 92–93
  eating disorders and, 12–13, 77, 80
  treatment of, 103–107
  warning signs of, 97–99, 107–109
Dexfenfluramine (Redux), 49–50
Diana, Princess of Wales, 69–70
diet drugs, 34, 40–41, 45, 127
  dietary supplements, 52–53
  herbal, 50–52
  over-the-counter, 46–47
  prescription, 48–50
  risks of, 46–48, 49, 50, 51, 53
diet industry, 42–43
dieting, 34, 43–44, 58
  health risks of, 34–35, 125
  success of, 43–44
diet shakes, 53–54
Dr. Atkins' Diet Revolution, 60

Dr. Stoll's Diet Aid, 53
"downers" (barbiturates), 48

E
eating disorders, 3, 12–13, 61, 66–70
  dangers of, 68
  depression and, 13–17
  symptoms of, 88–89
  treatment of, 85–88
electroconvulsive therapy (ECT), 106
endorphins, 83
ephedra (ma huang), 51
ephedrine, 51
exercise, 62–63, 123, 124
exercise addiction, 3, 82–84, 88–89

F
fad diets, 34, 61
fat-free foods, 56–57
firearms, 115, 116
fen-phen, 49–50, 51
Fonda, Jane, 69
Food and Drug Administration (FDA), 48, 50, 51, 52, 57, 71
Frazer, Brendan, 24–25

G
Ginger Spice (Geri Halliwell), 69
grapefruit diet, 61
gyms, 43, 63–64
gym equipment, 62, 64

H
Halliwell, Geri (Ginger
    Spice), 69
happiness, 6, 119
health clubs, 63–64
health food industry, 52
health food stores, 50
herbal fen-phen, 51
herbal weight-loss
    products, 59
high-protein diets, 60–61
hoarding, 79, 89

I
Ipecac, 79, 89

J
Jenny Craig, 55, 59

L
laxatives, 34, 89
liposuction, 65
low-carbohydrate diets,
    60–61
low-fat foods, 54–56

M
Madonna, 24
ma huang (ephedra), 51
men, eating disorders and,
    73, 86
Meridia, 48–49
Monroe, Marilyn, 23–24

N
National Association of
    Anorexia and

Associated Disorders
    (ANAD), 69
National Mental Health
    Association, 120
New England Journal of
    Medicine, 34–35, 125
Nutri/System, 55, 59

O
obesity, 13, 34–35
on-line help groups, 88
overachievers, 72, 127
Overeaters Anonymous
    (OA), 87–88
Olestra, 57–58
overweight, 2, 5–6, 26, 44

P
parents, 30–31, 91, 93–94,
    100–101
Paxil, 105
peer pressure, 11–12, 36
phenylpropanolamine
    (PPA), 46
prepackaged diet meals,
    42, 43, 55, 58–59
Prozac, 87, 105
Psychology Today, 20, 34
purging, 77, 78, 79

R
Redux (Dexfenfluramine),
    49–50, 51

S
saccharin, 56
The Scarsdale Diet, 60
Seasonal Affective Disorder

(SAD), 103
selective serotonin reuptake inhibitor (SSRI), 106
self-definition, 11
self-esteem, 126
serotonin, 49, 106
sex, unwanted, 36
sleep problems, 99, 114
smoking, 35, 55
"speed" (amphetamines), 47–48
standards of beauty, 22–25
staying positive, 120–121
St. John's Wort, 51
substance abuse, 36, 99, 120, 121
suicide, 3, 13, 94, 106, 110–111
   preventing, 115–117
   signals of, 111–115
supermodels, 21–22, 43

T
Tarzan, 24
teasing, 27–30
therapy, 104–105
trauma, 15, 16, 122–123
twelve-step programs, 86, 87

U
"uppers" (amphetamines, speed), 47–48

V
vomiting, 76, 78, 80

W
weight-loss and diet programs, 41, 58–59
Weight Watchers, 58–59
Weismuller, Johnny, 24–25
Wolf, Naomi, 69
working out, 63, 73

Y
yo-yo dieting, 34, 35, 82, 125

Z
Zoloft, 105
The Zone, 60